801 Action Verbs for Communicators

801 Action Verbs for Communicators

Position Yourself First with Action Verbs for Journalists, Speakers, Educators, Students, Resume-Writers, Editors & Travelers

Anne Hart

ASJA Press
New York Lincoln Shanghai

801 Action Verbs for Communicators
Position Yourself First with Action Verbs for Journalists, Speakers, Educators, Students, Resume-Writers, Editors & Travelers

ASJA Press
an imprint of iUniverse, Inc.

For information address:
iUniverse, Inc.
2021 Pine Lake Road, Suite 100
Lincoln, NE 68512
www.iuniverse.com

ISBN: 0-595-31911-4

Printed in the United States of America

Contents

801 Action Verbs for Communicators

1. Action verbs for communicators, career developers, educators, students, journalists, editors, job-seekers, travelers, resume-writers, novelists, and speakers. Position yourself with action verbs. Write resumes using action verbs for career advancement. Use action verbs for writing and journalism projects.

2. Action verbs in English, Spanish, French, Italian, German, Portuguese, and Russian. Write your resume or state your credentials in several languages.

3. Action Verbs for Communicators. Look up the verbs in several languages. Mix and match numbers to compare the verbs. Play word games. Use action verbs on your resume or in your writing or speaking to enhance your skills and action-verbs vocabulary. Use as verb games, for writing resumes, or communications.

Action Verbs
English

Action Verbs Used Frequently by Communicators

1. Arranged___
2. Asserted___
3. Assessed___
4. Budgeted___
5. Communicated___
6. Constructed___
7. Created___
8. Decided___
9. Demonstrated___
10. Designed___
11. Edited___
12. Encouraged___
13. Enriched___
14. Evaluated___
15. Expatiated___
16. Experienced___
17. Facilitated___
18. Implemented___
19. Improved___
20. Increased___
21. Indicated___
22. Inspired___
23. Integrated___
24. Initiated___
25. Instructed___
26. Interviewed___
27. Led___
28. Listened___
29. Motivated___
30. Negotiated___
31. Organized___
32. Planned___
33. Prepared___
34. Produced___
35. Promoted___
36. Published___
37. Researched___
38. Repaired___
39. Revised___
40. Sold___
41. Supervised___
42. Wrote___

801 Action Verbs for Communicators

1.	Abated	22.	Accounted
2.	Abbreviated	23.	Accredited
3.	Abstracted	24.	Accrued
4.	Abided	25.	Accumulated
5.	Abjured	26.	Accustomed
6.	Abridged	27.	Achieved
7.	Abrogated	28.	Acknowledged
8.	Abseiled	29.	Acquainted
9.	Absolved	30.	Acquired
10.	Abstained	31.	Acquitted
11.	Absorbed	32.	Acted
12.	Abstracted	33.	Activated
13.	Accepted	34.	Actualized
14.	Accelerated	35.	Adapted
15.	Acclaimed	36.	Adhered
16.	Accented	37.	Administered
17.	Accepted	38.	Adopted
18.	Acclimatized	39.	Advertised
19.	Accommodated	40.	Advised
20.	Accomplished	41.	Advocated
21.	Accorded	42.	Affected

43. Affirmed
44. Afforded
45. Agented
46. Agglutinated
47. Agreed
48. Aligned
49. Allocated
50. Amended
51. Analyzed
52. Anesthetized
53. Animated
54. Annotated
55. Announced
56. Anticipated
57. Appealed
58. Appeared
59. Applauded
60. Applied
61. Appliquéd
62. Appraised
63. Approved
64. Arbitrated

65. Archived
66. Argued
67. Arranged
68. Ascertained
69. Aspired
70. Assayed
71. Assembled
72. Asserted
73. Assessed
74. Assigned
75. Assimilated
76. Assisted
77. Associated
78. Assumed
79. Assured
80. Attached
81. Attained
82. Attended
83. Attributed
84. Attitudinized
85. Attuned
86. Audited

87. Audiodidacted

88. Audiotaped

89. Augmented

90. Authored

91. Authorize

92. Automated

93. Awarded

94. Became

95. Backed

96. Banked

97. Bartered

98. Beaded

99. Benchmarked

100. Benefited

101. Booked

102. Bought

103. Braided

104. Brailled

105. Branched

106. Breaded

107. Broadcasted

108. Brought

109. Budgeted

110. Built

111. Calculated

112. Calmed

113. Campaigned

114. Camped

115. Carded

116. Cared

117. Carried

118. Carted

119. Carved

120. Catalogued

121. Catapulted

122. Centered

123. Chaired

124. Changed

125. Channeled

126. Characterized

127. Charged

128. Charted

129. Chiseled

130. Cited

131. Civilized

132. Claimed

133. Clarified

134. Cleared

135. Clocked

136. Clued

137. Coached

138. Coded

139. Codified

140. Coifed

141. Collaborated

142. Collected

143. Colored

144. Commanded

145. Commemorated

146. Commercialized

147. Communicated

148. Compared

149. Competed

150. Compiled

151. Completed

152. Composed

153. Computed

154. Computerized

155. Conceived

156. Concentrated

157. Conceptualized

158. Conciliated

159. Conducted

160. Configured

161. Conquered

162. Conserved

163. Considered

164. Constructed

165. Construed

166. Consulted

167. Consumed

168. Contracted

169. Contributed

170. Controlled

171. Converged

172. Conversed

173. Cooperated

174. Co-opted

175. Coordinated

176. Copyrighted

177. Corded

178. Corrected

179. Correlated

180. Counseled

181. Counted

182. Courted

183. Created

184. Credited

185. Crewed

186. Critiqued

187. Crusaded

188. Cued

189. Cultured

190. Cut

191. Cycled

192. Dated

193. Davened

194. Dealt

195. Debited

196. Debriefed

197. Debugged

198. Decentralized

199. Decided

200. Deciphered

201. Declaimed

202. Declared

203. Decoded

204. Decorated

205. Decreased

206. Dedicated

207. Deferred

208. Defined

209. Deflected

210. Delegated

211. Deleted

212. Delineated

213. Delivered

214. Demonstrated

215. Demystified

216. Deprogrammed

217. Deregulated

218. Derived

219. Described

220. Designed

221. Detailed

222. Detected

223. Determined

224. Detoured

225. Developed

226. Devolved

227. Dined

228. Divided

229. Delighted

230. Devised

231. Devoted

232. Diagnosed

233. Dialogued

234. Diced

235. Dichotomized

236. Dictated

237. Differed

238. Digested

239. Digitized

240. Diluted

241. Directed

242. Digitized

243. Disagreed

244. Discovered

245. Discussed

246. Dispersed

247. Displayed

248. Dissolved

249. Distributed

250. Divided

251. Divined

252. Documented

253. Donated

254. Doused

255. Drafted

256. Drove

257. Edited

258. Educated

259. Effected

260. Effloresced

261. Eked out

262. Elaborated

263. Elasticized

264. Elbowed

265. Elected

266. Elegized

267. Elevated

268. Eliminated

269. Embroided

270. Emended

271. Emphasized

272. Employed

273. Empowered

274. Encountered

275. Encouraged

276. Energized

277. Engaged

278. Engineered

279. Engraved

280. Enhanced

281. Enlarged

282. Enlisted

283. Ensured

284. Entered

285. Entertained

286. Envisioned

287. Epigrammatized

288. Epitomized

289. Equalized

290. Erected

291. Eructed

292. Escorted

293. Established

294. Estimated

295. Etched

296. Etiolated

297. Eulogized

298. Euphemized

299. Evaluated

300. Evanesced

301. Evangelized

302. Evidenced

303. Evoked

304. Evolved

305. Exacerbated

306. Examined

307. Excavated

308. Excelled

309. Exchanged

310. Exclaimed

311. Excoriated

312. Exculpated

313. Executed

314. Exercised

315. Exhorted

316. Exfoliated

317. Exhibited

318. Exonerated

319. Exorcized

320. Expanded

321. Expatiated

322. Expedited

323. Experienced

324. Explained

325. Explored

326. Exported

327. Exposed

328. Expressed

329. Extended

330. Extrapolated

331. Facilitated

332. Farmed

333. Faxed

334. Federalized

335. Fertilized

336. Filed

337. Filled

338. Filmed

339. Financed

340. Fired

341. Fitted

342. Fixed

343. Fluctuated

344. Followed

345. Forecasted

346. Formalized

347. Formatted

348. Formed

349. Formulated

350. Fortified

351. Forwarded

352. Found

353. Founded

354. Franchised

355. Functioned

356. Furnished

357. Generated

358. Genealogized

359. Geneticized

360. Gestured

361. Gesticulated

362. Girded

363. Gnosticized

364. Governed

365. Graded

366. Granted

367. Graphed

368. Grew

369. Guaranteed

370. Guarded

371. Guided

372. Hafted

373. Handled

374. Harmonized

375. Headed

376. Healed

377. Helped

378. Hired

379. Humanized

380. Humored

381. Hypnotized

382. Identified

383. Ignited

384. Illustrated

385. Immigrated

386. Implanted

387. Implemented

388. Imported

389. Imposed

390. Impressed

391. Improved

392. Incited

393. Included

394. Incorporated

395. Increased

396. Indexed

397. Indicated

398. Indicted

399. Industrialized

400. Influenced

401. Informed

402. Initialized

403. Initiated

404. Inked

405. Inquired

406. Inspected

407. Inspired

408. Installed

409. Instituted

410. Instructed

411. Insured

412. Integrated

413. Interested

414. Interfaced

415. Internalized

416. Internationalized

417. Interpreted

418. Interviewed

419. Introduced

420. Intuited

421. Invested

422. Investigated

423. Invented

424. Inventoried

425. Inverted

426. Invested

427. Invigorated

428. Involved

429. Issued

430. Joined

431. Journalized

432. Journeyed

433. Judged

434. Juried

435. Justified

436. Keyboarded

437. Lamented

438. Laminated

439. Leased

440. Launched

441. Lectured

442. Legalized

443. Legitimized

444. Legislated

445. Lessened

446. Led

447. Left

448. Lighted

449. Linked

450. Litigated

451. Loaded

452. Loaned

453. Localized

454. Looked

455. Lyricized

456. Magnetized

457. Mailed

458. Maintained

459. Managed

460. Manipulated

461. Manufactured

462. Marketed

463. Mastered

464. Measured

465. Mediated

466. Memorized

467. Merchandised

468. Merged

469. Mesmerized

470. Met

471. Micrographed

472. Migrated

473. Ministered

474. Moderated

475. Modified

476. Modeled

477. Molded

478. Monitored

479. Morphed

480. Mortgaged

481. Motivated

482. Moved

483. Multicasted

484. Multiplied

485. Multitasked

486. Narrated

487. Navigated

488. Negotiated

489. Netcasted

490. Networked

491. Neutralized

492. Normalized

493. Normed

494. Notated

495. Noted

496. Notified

497. Notarized

498. Nursed

499. Obtained

500. Officiated

501. Opened

502. Orated

503. Operated

504. Opined

505. Orchestrated

506. Ordered

507. Organized

508. Oriented

509. Originated

510. Outlined

511. Outnumbered

512. Outpaced

513. Outperformed

514. Outran

515. Outshone

516. Outranked

517. Outvoted

518. Outwitted

519. Overawed

520. Overcame

521. Overdid

522. Overheard

523. Oversaw

524. Overstepped

525. Overstretched

526. Overwhelmed

527. Overworked

528. Overwrote

529. Owed

530. Owned

531. Oxygenated

532. Oxidized

533. Paced

534. Packaged

535. Packed

536. Parented

537. Participated

538. Partnered (with)

539. Patented

540. Patterned

541. Perceived

542. Performed

543. Personalized

544. Persuaded

545. Petitioned

546. Photocopied

547. Photographed

548. Piloted

549. Pinpointed

550. Planned

551. Planted

552. Played

553. Plotted

554. Pooled

555. Posed

556. Posted

557. Positioned

558. Practiced

559. Prayed

560. Predicted

561. Preempted

562. Prefaced

563. Preferred

564. Prepared

565. Presented

566. Presided

567. Pressed

568. Proceeded (to)

569. Processed

570. Procured

571. Produced

572. Professionalized

573. Programmed

574. Projected

575. Promoted

576. Proposed

577. Proofread

578. Protected

579. Protested

580. Protracted

581. Proved

582. Provided

583. Publicized

584. Published

585. Purchased

586. Qualified

587. Quantified

588. Quickened

589. Questioned

590. Queued

591. Quilted

592. Raised

593. Ran

594. Rated

595. Realized

596. Reaped

597. Reared

598. Reasoned

599. Recalled

600. Reclaimed

601. Recognized

602. Recommended

603. Reconciled

604. Reconstructed

605. Recorded

606. Recouped

607. Recovered

608. Recreated

609. Recruited

610. Rectified

611. Recycled

612. Redesigned

613. Redecorated

614. Reduced

615. Reenacted

616. Reentered

617. Referenced

618. Refreshed

619. Registered

620. Regulated

621. Rehired

622. Reimbursed

623. Reinforced

624. Related

625. Released

626. Relocated

627. Remedied

628. Reminisced

629. Remodeled

630. Renewed

631. Rented

632. Reoriented

633. Repaired

634. Replaced

635. Replenished

636. Reported

637. Represented

638. Required

639. Requisitioned

640. Researched

641. Resized

642. Reshaped

643. Resolved

644. Responded to

645. Restored

646. Resourced

647. Resulted

648. Retailed

649. Retained

650. Retrained

651. Retired

652. Retooled

653. Retrained

654. Retrieved

655. Returned

656. Reunited

657. Revamped

658. Reveled

659. Reviewed

660. Revised

661. Rewired

662. Roboticized

663. Rolled

664. Rotated

665. Routed

666. Rushed

667. Sailed

668. Sampled

669. Sanitized

670. Saved

671. Scanned

672. Scheduled

673. Scored

674. Screened

675. Scrimped

676. Sculptured

677. Sequenced

678. Selected

679. Sensed

680. Serialized

681. Served

682. Set objectives

683. Set up

684. Sewed

685. Shaped

686. Shared

687. Shredded

688. Showed

689. Simplified

690. Sized

691. Sold

692. Solicited

693. Solidified

694. Solved

695. Sorted

696. Sought

697. Specified

698. Spirited

699. Spoke

700. Sponsored

701. Spread

702. Staffed

703. Stabilized

704. Standardized

705. Starred

706. Stated

707. Stepped

708. Sterilized

709. Stimulated

710. Straightened

711. Streamlined

712. Strengthened

713. Stretched

714. Strolled

715. Strove

716. Structured

717. Styled

718. Subcontracted

719. Submitted

720. Succeeded

721. Summarized

722. Supervised

723. Supplied

724. Supported

725. Surfed

726. Surveyed

727. Survived

728. Syndicated

729. Synthesized

730. Systematized

731. Tabulated

732. Tamped

733. Taught

734. Taxed

735. Telecommuted

736. Telemarketed

737. Telephoned

738. Televised

739. Terminated

740. Tested

741. Thwarted

742. Told

743. Tolled

744. Toughened

745. Toured

746. Traced

747. Tracked

748. Traded

749. Trained

750. Transacted

751. Transcribed

752. Transferred

753. Translated

754. Transmitted

755. Transported

756. Treated

757. Troubleshot

758. Trucked

759. Truncated

760. Trusted

761. Typed

762. Typeset

763. Undertook

764. Unified

765. United

766. Updated

767. Upgraded

768. Underscored

769. Used

770. Utilized

771. Validated

772. Varied

773. Venerated

774. Verbalized

775. Verified

776. Videobiographed

777. Videographed

778. Videotaped

779. Viewed

780. Vindicated

781. Visualized

782. Vitalized

783. Vocalized

784. Voiced

785. Volunteered

786. Voted

787. Vulcanized

788. Waited

789. Waived

790. Wassailed

791. Weaned

792. Weighed

793. Weighted

794. Welded

795. Willed

796. Withdrew

797. Wholesaled

798. Won

799. Word processed

800. Worked

801. Wrote

Action Verbs
Spanish

Action Verbs in Spanish:
Frequently Used By Communicators
Verbos De la Acción: Verbos con frecuencia usados para los comunicadores y los reveladores de la carrera

1. Arreglado____
2. Afirmado____
3. Tasado____
4. Planeado el presupuesto____
5. Comunicado____
6. Construido____
7. Creado____
8. Decidido____
9. Demostrado____
10. Diseñado____
11. Corregido____
12. Animado____
13. Enriquecido____
14. Evaluado____
15. Extendido____
16. Experimentado____
17. Facilitado____
18. Puesto en práctica____
19. Mejorado____

20. Aumentado____
21. Indicado____
22. Inspirado____
23. Integrado____
24. Iniciado____
25. Instruido____
26. Entrevistado____
27. Conducido____
28. Escuchado____
29. Motivado____
30. Negociado____
31. Organizado____
32. Planeado____
33. Preparado____
34. Producido____
35. Promovido____
36. Publicado____
37. Investigado____
38. Reparado____

39. Revisado___

41. Supervisado___

40. Vendido___

42. Escribió___

801 Action Verbs in Spanish
Verbos de la acción para los comunicadores

1. Disminuido

18. Aclimatado

2. Abreviado

19. Acomodado

3. Abstraído

20. Dotado

4. Soportado

21. Concordado

5. Renunciado

22. Considerado

6. Condensado

23. Acreditado

7. Revocado

24. Aumentado

8. Hecho rappel

25. Acumulado

9. Exonerado

26. Acostumbrado

10. Abstenido

27. Conseguido

11. Absorbido

28. Reconocido

12. Abstraído

29. Informado

13. Aceptado

30. Adquirido

14. Acelerado

31. Absuelto

15. Aclamado

32. Interpretado

16. Acentuado

33. Activado

17. Aceptado

34. Actualizado

35. Adaptado
36. Adherido
37. Administrado
38. Adoptado
39. Anunciado
40. Aconsejado
41. Abogado
42. Afectado
43. Afirmado
44. Permitido
45. Agented
46. Aglutinado
47. Reconocido
48. Alineado
49. Asignado
50. Enmendado
51. Analizado
52. Anestesiado
53. Animado
54. Anotado
55. Anunciado
56. Esperado

57. Apelado
58. Parecido
59. Aplaudido
60. Aplicado
61. Appliquéd
62. Valorado
63. Aprobado
64. Arbitrado
65. Archivado
66. Argumentado
67. Arreglado
68. Averiguado
69. Aspirado
70. Assayed
71. Reunido
72. Afirmado
73. Tasado
74. Adjudicado
75. Asimilado
76. Asistido
77. Asociado
78. Asumido

79. Seguro

80. Atado

81. Alcanzado

82. Asistido

83. Atribuido

84. Attitudinized

85. Armonizado

86. Revisado

87. Audiodidacted

88. Audiotaped

89. Aumentado

90. Authored

91. Autorizar

92. Automatizado

93. Concedido

94. Se hizo

95. Apoyado

96. Depositado

97. Cambiado

98. Adornado con cuentas

99. Benchmarked

100. Beneficiado

101. Reservado

102. Comprado

103. Trenzado

104. Brailled

105. Bifurcado

106. Breaded

107. Transmitido

108. Traído

109. Planeado el presupuesto

110. Construido

111. Deliberado

112. Calmado

113. Hecho una campaña

114. Acampado

115. Carded

116. Preocupado

117. Llevado

118. Transportado

119. Esculpido

120. Catalogado

121. Lanzado

122. Centrado

123. Presidido

124. Cambiado

125. Canalizado

126. Caracterizado

127. Cargado

128. Charted

129. Esculpido

130. Citado

131. Civilizado

132. Reclamado

133. Clarificado

134. Limpiado

135. Cronometrado

136. Clued

137. Entrenado

138. Cifrado

139. Codificado

140. Pelo diseñado

141. Colaborado

142. Tranquilo

143. Coloreado

144. Mandado

145. Conmemorado

146. Comercializado

147. Comunicado

148. Comparado

149. Competido

150. Compilado

151. Completado

152. Tranquilo

153. Calculado

154. Automatizado

155. Concebido

156. Concentrado

157. Conceptuado

158. Apaciguado

159. Conducido

160. Configurado

161. Triunfado

162. Conservado

163. Considerado

164. Construido

165. Interpretado

166. Consultado

167. Consumido

168. Contratado

169. Contribuido

170. Controlado

171. Convergido

172. Dialogado

173. Cooperado

174. Cooptado

175. Coordinado

176. Copyrighted

177. Amarrado

178. Corregido

179. Correlacionado

180. Aconsejado

181. Contado

182. Solicitado

183. Creado

184. Creído

185. Tripulado

186. Critiqued

187. Hecho una cruzada

188. Cued

189. Cultivado

190. Corte

191. Cycled

192. Datado

193. Davened

194. Dado

195. Cargado en cuenta

196. Interrogado

197. Eliminado fallos

198. Descentralizado

199. Decidido

200. Descifrado

201. Recitado

202. Declarado

203. Descifrado

204. Decorado

205. Disminuido

206. Dedicado

207. Aplazado

208. Definido

209. Desviado

210. Delegado

211. Suprimido

212. Delineado

213. Entregado

214. Demostrado

215. Desmitificado

216. Deprogrammed

217. Desregulado

218. Sacado

219. Descrito

220. Diseñado

221. Detallado

222. Descubierto

223. Decidido

224. Desviado

225. Desarrollado

226. Delegado

227. Cenado

228. Dividido

229. Encantado

230. Ideado

231. Fiel

232. Diagnosticado

233. Dialogued

234. Jugado a los dados

235. Dichotomized

236. Dictado

237. Diferenciado

238. Digerido

239. Digitalizado

240. Diluido

241. Dirigido

242. Digitalizado

243. Discrepado

244. Descubierto

245. Hablado

246. Dispersado

247. Mostrado

248. Disuelto

249. Distribuido

250. Dividido

251. Adivinado

252. Documentado

253. Donado

254. Empapado

255. Redactado

256. Condujo

257. Corregido

258. Culto

259. Efectuado

260. Florecido

261. Estirado

262. Elaborado

263. Elasticized

264. Dado le un codazo

265. Decidido

266. Elegized

267. Elevado

268. Eliminado

269. Embroided

270. Enmendado

271. Enfatizado

272. Empleado

273. Autorizado

274. Encontrado

275. Animado

276. Activado

277. Ocupado

278. Tramado

279. Grabado

280. Realzado

281. Ampliado

282. Alistado

283. Asegurado

284. Entrado

285. Entretenido

286. Previsto

287. Epigrammatized

288. Personificado

289. Igualado

290. Erigido

291. Eructed

292. Escoltado

293. Establecido

294. Estimado

295. Grabado

296. Etiolated

297. Elogiado

298. Euphemized

299. Evaluado

300. Evanesced

301. Evangelizado

302. Evidenciado

303. Evocado

304. Desarrollado

305. Exacerbado

306. Examinado

307. Excavado

308. Excelled

309. Cambiado

310. Gritado

311. Excoriated

312. Exculpado

313. Ejecutado

314. Ejercido

315. Exhortado

316. Exfoliated

317. Expuesto

318. Exonerado

319. Exorcizado

320. Dilatado

321. Extendido

322. Acelerado

323. Experimentado

324. Explicado

325. Explorado

326. Exportado

327. Expuesto

328. Expresado

329. Ampliado

330. Extrapolado

331. Facilitado

332. Cultivado

333. Mandado por fax

334. Federalizado

335. Fertilizado

336. Archivado

337. Lleno

338. Filmado

339. Financiado

340. Encendido

341. Empotrado

342. Fijo

343. Fluctuado

344. Seguido

345. Pronosticado

346. Formalizado

347. Formateado

348. Formado

349. Formulado

350. Fortificado

351. Expedido

352. Encontrado

353. Fundado

354. Concesionario

355. Funcionado

356. Amueblado

357. Generado

358. Genealogized

359. Analizado por genética

360. Gestured

361. Gesticulado

362. Ceñido

363. Gnosticized

364. Gobernado

365. Clasificado

366. Concedido

367. Gráfico

368. Creció

369. Garantizado

370. Cauteloso

371. Dirigido

372. Hafted

373. Manejado

374. Armonizado

375. Encabezado

376. Curado

377. Ayudado

378. Alquilado

379. Humanizado

380. Humored

381. Hipnotizado

382. Identificado

383. Encendido

384. Ilustrado

385. Inmigrado

386. Implantado

387. Puesto en práctica

388. Importado

389. Impuesto

390. Impresionado

391. Mejorado

392. Incitado

393. Incluido

394. Incorporado

395. Aumentado

396. Puesto índice

397. Indicado

398. Procesado

399. Industrializado

400. Influido

401. Informado

402. Inicializado

403. Iniciado

404. Ilustrado con la tinta

405. Preguntado

406. Inspeccionado

407. Inspirado

408. Instalado

409. Instituido

410. Instruido

411. Asegurado

412. Integrado

413. Interesado

414. Interafrontado

415. Interiorizado

416. Internacionalizado

417. Interpretado

418. Entrevistado

419. Introducido

420. Intuited

421. Invertido

422. Investigado

423. Inventado

424. Inventoried

425. Invertido

426. Invertido

427. Tonificante

428. Complicado

429. Publicado

430. Unido

431. Asentado en el libro diario

432. Viajado

433. Juzgado

434. Servido sobre jurados

435. Justificado

436. Escrito a máquina

437. Llorado

438. Laminado

439. Arrendado

440. Lanzado

441. Sermoneado

442. Legalizado

443. Legitimado

444. Legislado

445. Disminuido

446. Conducido

447. Dejado

448. Encendido

449. Unido

450. Pleiteado

451. Cargado

452. Prestado

453. Loca

454. Mirado

455. Líricas creadas

456. Magnetizado

457. Enviado

458. Mantenido

459. Manejado

460. Manipulado

461. Fabricado

462. Marketed

463. Dominado

464. Moderado

465. Mediado

466. Memorizado

467. Comerciado

468. Combinado

469. Hipnotizado

470. Encontrado

471. Micrográfico

472. Emigrado

473. Ministro ayudado

474. Moderado

475. Modificado

476. Modelado

477. Moldeado

478. Supervisado

479. Morphed

480. Hipotecado

481. Motivado

482. Movido

483. Multicasted

484. Multiplicado

485. Multitasked

486. Relatado

487. Navegado

488. Negociado

489. Netcasted

490. Conectado a una red

491. Neutralizado

492. Normalizado

493. Normed

494. Notado

495. Digno de nota

496. Notificado

497. Escriturado

498. Cuidado

499. Obtenido

500. Ejercido

501. Abierto

502. Orado

503. Hecho funcionar

504. Opinado

505. Orquestado

506. Ordenado

507. Organizado

508. Orientado

509. Originado

510. Perfilado

511. Superado en número

512. Dejado atrás

513. Superado

514. Excedió

515. Eclipsado

516. Excedido en grado

517. Vencido en una votación

518. Burlado

519. Intimidado

520. Venció

521. Exageró

522. Oído por casualidad

523. Supervisó

524. Sobrepasado

525. Sobreestirado

526. Abrumado

527. Forzado

528. Superpuso

529. Debido

530. Poseído

531. Oxigenado

532. Oxidado

533. Marcado el paso

534. Embalado

535. Embalado

536. Actuado como padre

537. Participado

538. Acompañado (con)

539. Patentado

540. Decorado

541. Percibido

542. Realizado

543. Personalizado

544. Persuadido

545. Presentado una solicitud

546. Fotocopiado

547. Fotografiado

548. Pilotado

549. Señalado

550. Planeado

551. Plantado

552. Jugado

553. Trazado

554. Reunido

555. Planteado

556. Fijado

557. Colocado

558. Experto

559. Rezado

560. Predicho

561. Adelantado

562. Introducido

563. Preferido

564. Preparado

565. Presentado

566. Presidido

567. Embutido

568. Procedido (a)

569. Tratado

570. Conseguido

571. Producido

572. Trabajar profesionalmente

573. Programado

574. Proyectado

575. Promovido

576. Propuesto

577. Corregido las pruebas

578. Protegido

579. Protestado

580. Prolongado

581. Probado

582. A condición de que

583. Hecho público

584. Publicado

585. Comprado

586. Calificado

587. Cuantificado

588. Acelerado

589. Preguntado

590. Colocado en fila

591. Acolchado

592. Levantado

593. Corrió

594. Nominal

595. Realizado

596. Cosechado

597. Criado

598. Razonado

599. Recordado

600. Reclamado

601. Aprobado

602. Recomendado

603. Reconciliado

604. Reconstruido

605. Registrado

606. Recuperado

607. Recuperado

608. Recreado

609. Reclutado

610. Rectificado

611. Reciclado

612. Diseñado

613. Repintado

614. Reducido

615. Decretado de nuevo

616. Entrado de nuevo

617. Referido

618. Refrescado

619. Certificado

620. Regulado

621. Alquilado de nuevo

622. Reembolsado

623. Reforzado

624. Relacionado

625. Liberado

626. Trasladado

627. Remediado

628. Rememorado

629. Remodelado

630. Renovado

631. Alquilado

632. Reorientado

633. Reparado

634. Sustituido

635. Rellenado

636. Relatado

637. Representado

638. Requerido

639. Requisado

640. Researche

641. Cambiado el tamaño

642. Reformado

643. Resuelto

644. Respondido a

645. Restaurado

646. Recursos buscados

647. Resultado

648. Vendido al por menor

649. Retenido

650. Reciclado

651. Jubilado

652. Re-fileteado

653. Reciclado

654. Recuperado

655. Devuelto

656. Reunido

657. Renovado

658. Divertido

659. Examinado

660. Revisado

661. Reconectado

662. Mejorado a robots

663. Hecho rodar

664. Hecho girar

665. Derrotado

666. Apresurado

667. Navegado

668. Probado

669. Esterilizado

670. Salvado

671. Explorado

672. Previsto

673. Marcado

674. Protegido

675. Escatimado

676. Esculpido

677. Ordenado

678. Seleccionado

679. Sentido

680. Seriado

681. Servido

682. Objetivos de juego

683. Establecido

684. Cosido

685. Formado

686. Compartido

687. Triturado

688. Mostró

689. Simplificado

690. Clasificado

691. Vendido

692. Solicitado

693. Solidificado

694. Solucionado

695. Clasificado

696. Buscado

697. Especificado

698. Animado

699. Habló

700. Patrocinado

701. Extensión

702. Proveído de personal

703. Estabilizado

704. Estandartizado

705. Estrellado

706. Indicado

707. Andado

708. Esterilizado

709. Estimulado

710. Enderezado

711. Aerodinamizado

712. Reforzado

713. Estirado

714. Paseado

715. Se esforzó

716. Estructurado

717. Diseñado

718. Subcontratado

719. Presentado

720. Logrado

721. Resumido

722. Supervisado

723. Suministrado

724. Apoyado

725. Hecho surf

726. Contemplado

727. Sobrevivido

728. Sindicado

729. Sintetizado

730. Sistematizado

731. Tabulado

732. Apisonado

733. Enseñado

734. Cobrado los impuestos

735. Trabajado en el país

736. Puesto por el teléfono

737. Llamado por teléfono

738. Televisado

739. Terminado

740. Probado

741. Frustrado

742. Dicho

743. Tañido

744. Endurecido

745. Recorrido

746. Remontado

747. Rastreado

748. Cambiado

749. Entrenado

750. Despachado

751. Transcrito

752. Transferido

753. Traducido

754. Transmitido

755. Transportado

756. Tratado

757. Solucionado

758. Condujo camiones

759. Truncado

760. Confiado

761. Escrito a máquina

762. Componer

763. Emprendió

764. Unificado

765. Unido

766. Actualizado

767. Mejorado

768. Subrayado

769. Usado

770. Utilizado

771. Validado

772. Variado

773. Venerado

774. Expresado con palabras

775. Verificado

776. Biografías grabadas

777. Vídeo gráfico gráficamente

778. Grabado en vídeo

779. Visto

780. Justificado

781. Visualizado

782. Vitalizado

783. Vocalizado

784. Expresado

785. Ofrecido

786. Votado

787. Vulcanizado

788. Esperado

789. Renunciado

790. Honrado

791. Destetado

792. Pesado

793. Ponderado

794. Soldado

795. Testamentos consultados

796. Se retiró

797. Venta al por mayor dada

798. Ganado

799. Palabra tratada

800. Trabajado

801. Escribió

Action Verbs
French

Action Verbs in French Frequently Used by Communicators

Verbes D'Action: Verbes fréquemment utilisés pour des communicateurs et des lotisseurs de carrière

1. Arrangé___
2. Affirmé___
3. Imposé___
4. Budgétisé___
5. Communiqué___
6. Construit___
7. Créé___
8. Décidé___
9. Démontré___
10. Conçu___
11. Edité___
12. Encouragé___
13. Enrichi___
14. Evalué___
15. Disserté___
16. Expérimenté___
17. Facilité___
18. Appliqué___
19. Amélioré___
20. Augmenté___
21. Indiqué___
22. Inspiré___
23. Intégré___
24. Inauguré___
25. Instruit___
26. Interviewé___
27. Mené___
28. Ecouté___
29. Motivé___
30. Négocié___
31. Organisé___
32. Planifié___
33. Préparé___
34. Produit___
35. Promu___
36. Publié___
37. Préparé___
38. Réparé___

39. Révisé___	41. Surveillé___
40. Vendu___	42. A écrit___

801 Action Verbs in French
Verbes d'action pour des communicateurs
Verbes D'Action

1. Diminué	17. Admis
2. Abrégé	18. Acclimaté
3. Soustrait	19. Adapté
4. Demeuré	20. Accompli
5. Abjuré	21. Accordé
6. Abrégé	22. A rendu compte
7. Abrogé	23. Accrédité
8. Abseiled	24. Accru
9. Affranchi	25. Accumulé
10. Abstenu	26. Accoutumé
11. Absorbé	27. Réalisé
12. Soustrait	28. Reconnu
13. Admis	29. Au courant
14. Accéléré	30. Acquis
15. Acclamé	31. Acquitté
16. Accentué	32. Agi

33. Activé

34. Actualisé

35. Adapté

36. Adhéré

37. Administré

38. Adopté

39. Annoncé

40. Conseillé

41. Préconisé

42. Affecté

43. Affirmé

44. Eu les moyens

45. Agented

46. Agglutiné

47. Convenu

48. Aligné

49. Assigné

50. Modifié

51. Analysé

52. Anesthésié

53. Animé

54. Annoté

55. Annoncé

56. Prévu

57. En appelés

58. Apparus.

59. Applaudi

60. Appliqué

61. Appliquéd

62. Évalué

63. Approuvé

64. Arbitré

65. Archivé

66. Discuté

67. Disposé

68. Assuré

69. Aspiré

70. Analysé

71. Réuni

72. Affirmé

73. Évalué

74. Assigné

75. Assimilé

76. Aidé

77. Associé

78. Assumé

79. Assuré

80. Attaché

81. Atteint

82. Présent

83. Attribué

84. Attitudinized

85. Adapté

86. Apuré

87. Audiodidacted

88. Audiotaped

89. Augmenté

90. Écrit

91. Autorisez

92. Automatisé

93. Attribué

94. Est devenu

95. Soutenu

96. Encaissé

97. Échangé

98. Perlé

99. Benchmarked

100. Bénéficié

101. Réservé

102. Acheté

103. Tressé

104. A écrit dans braille

105. Embranché

106. Pané

107. Annoncé

108. Apporté

109. Économisé

110. Construit

111. Calculé

112. Calmé

113. Fait campagne

114. Campé

115. Cardé

116. Inquiété

117. Porté

118. Transporté en charrette

119. Découpé

120. Catalogué

121. Catapulté

122. Centré

123. Présidé

124. Changé

125. Creusé des rigoles

126. Caractérisé

127. Chargé

128. Dressé une carte

129. Ciselé

130. Cité

131. Civilisé

132. Réclamé

133. Clarifié

134. Dégagé

135. Synchronisé

136. Clued

137. Donné des leçons particulières

138. Codé

139. Codifié

140. Coifed

141. Collaboré

142. Rassemblé

143. Coloré

144. Commandé

145. Commémoré

146. Commercialisé

147. Communiqué

148. Comparé

149. Concurrencé

150. Compilé

151. Accompli

152. Composé

153. Calculé

154. Automatisé

155. Conçu

156. Concentré

157. Conceptualisé

158. Concilié

159. Conduit

160. Configuré

161. Conquis

162. Conservé

163. Considéré

164. Construit

165. Interprété

166. Consultant

167. Consommé

168. Contracté

169. Contribué

170. Commandé

171. Convergé

172. Conversé

173. Coopéré

174. Coopté

175. Coordonnés

176. Garanti les droits d'auteur

177. Attachés

178. Corrigé

179. Corrélé

180. Conseillé

181. Compté

182. Allé au devant

183. Créé

184. Crédité

185. Crewed

186. Critiqued

187. Crusaded

188. Positionné

189. Cultivé

190. Coupe

191. Fait un cycle

192. Daté

193. Davened

194. Occupé

195. Débité

196. Fait faire un compte rendu

197. Corrigé

198. Décentralisé

199. Décidé

200. Déchiffré

201. Déclamé

202. Avoué

203. Décodés

204. Décoré

205. Diminué

206. Consacré

207. Reporté

208. Defines

209. Délégué

210. Guidés

211. Supprimé

212. Tracé

213. Livré

214. Démontré

215. Demystified

216. Deprogrammed

217. Déréglé

218. Dérivé

219. Décrit

220. Conçu

221. Détaillé

222. Détecté

223. Déterminé

224. Dévié

225. Développé

226. Incombé

227. Diné

228. Divisé

229. Ravi

230. Conçu

231. Consacré

232. Diagnostiqué

233. Dialogué

234. Découpé

235. Dichotomisé

236. Dicté

237. Différé

238. Digéré

239. Digitalisé

240. Dilué

241. Dirigé

242. Digitalisé

243. Été en désaccord

244. Découvert

245. Discuté

246. Dispersé

247. Montré

248. Dissous

249. Distribué

250. Divisé

251. Deviné

252. Documenté

253. Donné

254. Trempé

255. Rédigé

256. A conduit

257. Édité

258. Instruit

259. Effectué

260. Effloresced

261. Suppléé à l'insuffisance hors de

262. Élaboré

263. Elasticized

264. Écarté d'un coup de coude

265. Élu

266. Elegized

267. Élevé

268. Éliminé

269. Embroided

270. Modifié

271. Souligné

272. Utilisé

273. Autorisé

274. Rencontré

275. Encouragé

276. Activé

277. Engagé

278. Machiné

279. Gravé

280. Augmenté

281. Agrandi

282. Enrôlé

283. Assuré

284. Entré

285. Amusé

286. Envisagé

287. Epigrammatized

288. Résumé

289. Égalisé

290. Érigé

291. Eructed

292. Escorté

293. Établi

294. Estimé

295. Gravé à l'eau-forte

296. Etiolated

297. Loué

298. Euphemized

299. Évalué

300. Bouillonné

301. Évangélisé

302. Démontré

303. Évoqué

304. Évolué

305. Aggravé

306. Examiné

307. Excavé

308. Excelé

309. Échangé

310. Hurlé

311. Excorié

312. Disculpé

313. Exécuté

314. Exercé

315. Recommandé instamment

316. Exfoliated

317. Exhibé

318. Acquitté

319. Exorcizé

320. Augmenté

321. Expatiated

322. Expédié

323. Expérimenté

324. Expliqué

325. Exploré

326. Exporté

327. Exposé

328. Exprimé

329. Prolongé

330. Extrapolé

331. Facilité

332. Cultivé

333. Envoyé par fax

334. Federalized

335. Fertilisé

336. Classé

337. Rempli

338. Filmé

339. Financé

340. Mis le feu

341. Adapté

342. Fixe

343. Flotté

344. Suivi

345. Prévu

346. Formalisé

347. Composé

348. Formé

349. Formulé

350. Enrichi

351. Expédié

352. Trouvé

353. Fondé

354. Concessionnaire

355. Fonctionné

356. Meublé

357. Produit

358. Genealogized

359. Geneticized

360. Fait des gestes

361. Gesticulé

362. Enserré

363. Gnosticized

364. Régi

365. Évalué

366. Accordé

367. Représenté graphiquement

368. S'est développé

369. Garanti

370. Gardé

371. Guidé

372. Hafted

373. Manipulé

374. Harmonisé

375. Dirigé

376. Guéri

377. Aidé

378. Loué

379. Humanisé

380. Câliné

381. Hypnotisé

382. Identifié

383. Mis à feu

384. Illustré

385. Immigré

386. Implanté

387. Mis en application

388. Importé

389. Imposé

390. Appliqué

391. Amélioré

392. Incité

393. Inclus

394. Incorporé

395. Accru

396. Classé

397. Indiqué

398. Accusé

399. Industrialisé

400. Influencé

401. Au courant

402. Initialisé

403. Lancé

404. Encré

405. Enquis

406. Inspecté

407. Inspiré

408. Installé

409. Institué

410. Instruit

411. Assurés

412. Intégré

413. Intéressé

414. Connecté

415. Internalisés

416. Internationalisé

417. Interprété

418. Interviewé

419. Présenté

420. Intuited

421. Investi

422. Étudié

423. Inventé

424. Inventorié

425. Inversé

426. Investi

427. Fortifié

428. Impliqué

429. Publié

430. Jointif

431. Écrit

432. Voyagé

433. Jugé

434. Juried

435. Justifié

436. Introduit au clavier

437. Déploré

438. Stratifié

439. Loué

440. Lancé

441. Parlé

442. Légalisé

443. Légitimé

444. Légiféré

445. Diminué

446. Mené

447. Gauche

448. Allumé

449. Lié

450. Plaidé

451. Chargé

452. Prêté

453. Localisé

454. Regardé

455. Lyrique

456. Magnétisé

457. Expédié

458. Maintenu

459. Contrôlé

460. Manoeuvré

461. Manufacturé

462. Lancé sur le marché

463. Maîtrisé

464. Mesuré

465. Négocié

466. Appris par coeur

467. Vendu

468. Fusionné

469. Hypnotisé

470. Réuni

471. Micrographed

472. Émigré

473. Ministre

474. Modéré

475. Modifié

476. Modelé

477. Moulé

478. Surveillé

479. Métamorphosé

480. Hypothèqué

481. Motivé

482. Déplacé

483. Annoncé sur l'Internet et d'autres médias

484. Multiplié

485. Multitasked

486. Relaté

487. Dirigé

488. Négocié

489. Netcasted

490. Géré en réseau

491. Neutralisé

492. Calculé pour normaliser

493. A figuré la norme

494. A écrit dans les notes musicales

495. Remarquable

496. Annoncé

497. Fait certifier devant notaire

498. Nourri

499. Obtenu

500. Officié

501. Ouvert

502. Rai en tant qu'orateur

503. Fonctionné

504. Été d'avis

505. Orchestré

506. Passé commande

507. Organisé

508. Orienté

509. D'origine

510. Décrit

511. Dépassé en nombre

512. Dépassé

513. Surpassé

514. Dépassé

515. Plus lumineux poli

516. Rangé plus fortement

517. Battu aux voix

518. Surpassé

519. Au-dessus d'intimidé

520. A surmonté

521. A exagéré

522. A surpris

523. A surveillé

524. A outrepassé

525. Surétendu

526. Accablé

527. Surchargé

528. A recouvert

529. Dû

530. Possédé

531. Oxygéné

532. Oxydé

533. Entraîné

534. Emballé

535. Emballé

536. Parented

537. Participé

538. A acquis un associé avec

539. Breveté

540. Modelé

541. Perçu

542. Exécuté

543. Personnalisé

544. Persuadé

545. Pétitionné

546. Photocopié

547. Photographié

548. Piloté

549. Indiqué exactement

550. Prévu

551. Planté

552. Joué

553. Tracé

554. Mis en commun

555. Posé

556. Signalé

557. Placé

558. Pratiqué

559. Prié

560. Prévu

561. Acquis

562. Préfacé

563. Préféré

564. Préparé

565. Présenté

566. Présidé

567. Serré

568. (à) procédés

569. Traité

570. Obtenu

571. Produit

572. Professionalized

573. Programmé

574. Projeté

575. Favorisé

576. Proposé

577. Corrigé

578. Protégé

579. Protesté

580. Prolongé

581. Avéré

582. Fourni

583. Annoncé

584. Édité

585. Acheté

586. Qualifié

587. Mesuré

588. Activé

589. Interrogé

590. Aligné

591. Piqué

592. Augmenté

593. A couru

594. Évalué

595. Réalisé

596. Récolté

597. Élevé

598. Raisonné

599. Rappelé

600. Repris

601. Reconnu

602. Recommandé

603. Réconcilié

604. Reconstruit

605. Enregistré

606. Récupéré

607. Récupéré

608. Recréé

609. Recruté

610. Rectifié

611. Réutilisé

612. Remodelé

613. Redecorated

614. Réduit

615. Reenacted

616. Réintroduit

617. Référencé

618. Régénéré

619. Enregistré

620. Réglé

621. Rehired

622. Remboursé

623. Renforcé

624. Connexe

625. Libéré

626. Replacé

627. Remédié à

628. Rappelé

629. Transformé

630. Remplacé

631. Loué

632. Réorienté

633. Réparé

634. Remplacé

635. Complété le niveau

636. Rapporté

637. Représenté

638. Requis

639. Réquisitionné

640. Recherché

641. Remis à la côte

642. Remodelé

643. Résolu

644. Répondu à

645. Reconstitué

646. Resourced

647. Résulté

648. Vendu au détail

649. Maintenu

650. Recyclé

651. Retiré

652. Usiné

653. Recyclé

654. Recherché

655. Retourné

656. Réuni

657. Amélioré

658. Reveled

659. Passé en revue

660. Révisé

661. De câble encore

662. Amélioré aux robots

663. Roulé

664. Tourné

665. Conduit

666. Précipité

667. Navigué

668. Prélevé

669. Aseptisé

670. Économisé

671. Balayé

672. Programmé

673. Marqué

674. Examiné

675. Lésiné

676. Sculpté

677. Ordonnancé

678. Choisi

679. Senti

680. Arrangé en série

681. Servi

682. Définissez les objectifs

683. Installé

684. Cousu

685. Formé

686. Partagé

687. Déchiqueté

688. Montré

689. Simplifié

690. Classé

691. Vendu

692. Sollicité

693. Solidifié

694. Résolu

695. Assorti

696. Cherché

697. Indiqué

698. Avec l'esprit

699. Rai

700. Commandité

701. Diffusion

702. Fourni de personnel

703. Stabilisé

704. Normalisé

705. Mis en lumière dedans

706. Indiqué

707. Fait un pas

708. Stérilisé

709. Stimulé

710. Redressé

711. Profilé

712. Renforcé

713. Étiré

714. Flâné

715. A tâché

716. Structuré

717. Dénommé

718. Sous-traité

719. Soumis

720. Réussi

721. Récapitulé

722. Dirigé

723. Fourni

724. Soutenu

725. Surfé

726. Examiné

727. Survécu

728. Envoyé dans le syndication

729. Synthétisé

730. Systématisé

731. Sous forme de tableaux

732. Martelé

733. Enseigné

734. Imposé

735. Travaillé de la maison

736. Lancé sur le marché par téléphone

737. Téléphoné

738. Télévisé

739. Terminé

740. Examiné

741. Contrecarré

742. Le dit

743. Sonné

744. Durçi

745. Voyagé

746. Tracé

747. Dépisté

748. Commercé

749. Exercé

750. Traité

751. Transcrit

752. Transféré

753. Traduit

754. Transmis

755. Transporté

756. Traité

757. Dépanné

758. Troqué

759. Tronqué

760. Fait confiance

761. Dactylographié

762. Composé

763. A entrepris

764. Unifié

765. Uni

766. Mis à jour

767. Amélioré

768. Souligné

769. Utilisé

770. Utilisé

771. Validé

772. Divers

773. Venerated

774. Verbalized

775. Vérifié

776. J'ai enregistré des biographies en vidéo

777. Attaché du ruban adhésif sur la vidéo

778. Enregistré en vidéo

779. Vu

780. Défendu

781. Visualisé

782. Animé

783. Exprimé

784. Exprimé

785. Offert

786. Voté

787. Vulcanisé

788. Attendu

789. Écarté

790. Salué avec une boisson

791. Sevré

792. Pesé

793. Pesé

794. Soudé

795. Voulu

796. S'est retiré

797. Vendu en gros

798. Gagné

799. Le mot a traité

800. Travaillé

801. A écrit

Action Verbs
Italian

Action Verbs in Italian—
Frequently Used by Communicators
Verbi Di Azione: Verbi frequentemente usati per i trasmettitori e gli sviluppatori di carriera

1. Organizzato___

2. Asserito___

3. Valutato___

4. ___stanziato

5. Comunicato___

6. Costruito___

7. Generato___

8. Deciso___

9. Dimostrato___

10. Progettato___

11. Pubblicato___

12. Consigliato a___

13. Arricchito___

14. ___valutato

15. ___di Expatiated

16. Con esperienza___

17. Facilitato___

18. Effettuato___

19. Migliorato___

20. Aumentato___

21. Indicato___

22. Ispirato___

23. Integrato___

24. Iniziato___

25. Insegnato a___

26. Intervistato___

27. Condotto___

28. Ascoltato___

29. Motivato___

30. Negoziato___

31. Organizzato___

32. Previsto___

33. Preparato___

34. Prodotto___

35. Promosso___

36. Pubblicato___

37. Ricercato___

38. Riparato___

39.   ___modificato

40.   Venduto___

41.   Sorvegliato___

42.   Ha scritto il___

801 Action Verbs in Italian
Verbi di azione per i trasmettitori

1.   Ridotto

2.   Abbreviato

3.   Sottratto

4.   Rimasto

5.   Abiurato

6.   Ridotto

7.   Abrogated

8.   Abseiled

9.   Assolto

10.   Astenuto

11.   Assorbito

12.   Sottratto

13.   Accettato

14.   Accelerare

15.   Applaudito

16.   Accentato

17.   Accettato

18.   Acclimatato

19.   Accomodato

20.   Compiuto

21.   Conciliato

22.   Ha spiegato

23.   Accreditato

24.   Accresciuto

25.   Accumulato

26.   Abituato

27.   Realizzato

28.   Riconosciuto

29.   Al corrente

30.   Acquistato

31.   Saldato

32.   Comportato

33.   Attivato

34.   Attualizzato

35. Adattato	57. Fatti appello
36. Aderito	58. Comparsi
37. Amministrato	59. Applaudito
38. Adottato	60. Applicato
39. Fatto pubblicità a	61. Appliquéd
40. Raccomandato	62. Valutato
41. Sostenuto	63. Approvato
42. Riguardato	64. Arbitrato
43. Affermato	65. Archiviato
44. Permesso	66. Discusso
45. Agented	67. Organizzato
46. Agglutinato	68. Accertato
47. Stato conforme	69. Aspirato
48. Allineato	70. Analizzato
49. Assegnato	71. Montato
50. Emendato	72. Asserito
51. Analizzato	73. Valutato
52. Anestetizzato	74. Assegnato
53. Animato	75. Assimilato
54. Annotato	76. Aiutato
55. Annunciato	77. Collegato
56. Anticipato	78. Presupposto

79. Assicurato
80. Fissato
81. Raggiunto
82. Assistito
83. Attribuito
84. Attitudinized
85. Adattato
86. Verificato
87. Audiodidacted
88. Audiotaped
89. Aumentato
90. Creato
91. Autorizzi
92. Automatizzato
93. Assegnato
94. È diventato
95. Sostenuto
96. Contato
97. Barattato
98. In rilievo
99. Benchmarked
100. Avvantaggiato
101. Prenotato
102. Comprato
103. Braided
104. Scritto in Braille
105. Ramificato
106. Impanato
107. Trasmesso per radio
108. Portato
109. Stanziato
110. Costruito
111. Calcolato
112. Calmato
113. Fatto una campagna
114. Accampato
115. Cardato
116. Preoccupato
117. Trasportato
118. Carted
119. Intagliato
120. Catalogato
121. Catapulted
122. Concentrato

123. Presieduto

124. Variabile

125. Scavato canali

126. Caratterizzato

127. Caricato

128. Progettato

129. Cesellato

130. Citato

131. Civilizzato

132. Sostenuto

133. Chiarito

134. Eliminato

135. Cronometrato

136. Pornito gli indizii

137. Istruito

138. Codificato

139. Codificato

140. Coifed

141. Collaborato

142. Raccolto

143. Colorato

144. Comandato

145. Commemorato

146. Commercializzato

147. Comunicato

148. Confrontato

149. Competuto

150. Compilato

151. Completato

152. Composto

153. Computato

154. Automatizzato

155. Concepito

156. Concentrato

157. Concettualizzato

158. Conciliato

159. Condotto

160. Configurato

161. Conquistato

162. Conservato

163. Considerato

164. Costruito

165. Inteso

166. Di consulenza

167. Consumato

168. Contratto

169. Contribuito

170. Controllato

171. Convergente

172. Conversato

173. Cooperato

174. Co-opted

175. Coordinati

176. Diritti editoriali registrati

177. Corretto

178. Spostato con cavo

179. Correlato

180. Consigliato

181. Contato

182. Sollecitato

183. Generato

184. Accreditato

185. Crewed

186. Critiqued

187. Crusaded

188. Indicazioni offerte

189. Coltivato

190. Taglio

191. Ciclato

192. Ora e giorno corretti registrati

193. Davened

194. Trattato

195. Addebitato

196. Istruzione rimossa

197. Messo a punto

198. Decentralizzato

199. Deciso

200. Decifrato

201. Declaimed

202. Dichiarato

203. Decorato

204. Decodificati

205. Diminuito

206. Dedicato

207. Rinviato

208. Delegato

209. Definiti

210. Deviati

211. Cancellato

212. Delineato

213. Trasportato

214. Dimostrato

215. Mistero rimosso

216. Programmazione rimossa

217. Diregolarizzato

218. Derivato

219. Descritto

220. Progettato

221. Dettagliato

222. Rilevato

223. Risoluto

224. Detoured

225. Sviluppato

226. Devoluto

227. Pranzato

228. Diviso

229. Contentissimo

230. Inventato

231. Dedicato con emozione

232. Diagnosticato

233. Dialogato

234. Tagliato

235. Diviso

236. Dettato

237. Differito da

238. Digerito

239. Dato valori numerici a

240. Diluito

241. Diretto

242. Dato valori numerici a

243. Non stato d'accordo

244. Scoperto

245. Discusso

246. Disperso

247. Visualizzato

248. Dissolto

249. Distribuito

250. Diviso

251. Generato da divinity

252. Documentato

253. Donato

254. Acqua individuata con l'intuizione

255. Disegnato

256. Ha guidato

257. Pubblicato

258. Istruito

259. Effettuato

260. Effloresced

261. Eked verso l'esterno

262. Elaborato

263. Elastico fatto

264. Gomiti usati

265. Scelto

266. Elegized

267. Elevato

268. Eliminato

269. Embroided

270. Emendato

271. Dato risalto a

272. Impiegato

273. Autorizzato

274. Incontrato

275. Consigliato a

276. Eccitato

277. Agganciato

278. Costruito

279. Inciso

280. Aumentato

281. Ingrandito

282. Arruolato

283. Accertato

284. Entrato

285. Intrattenuto

286. Previsto

287. Epigrammatized

288. Ha fatto l'epitome

289. Livellato

290. Eretto

291. Vento espulso dalla bocca

292. Accompagnato

293. Stabilito

294. Valutato

295. Inciso

296. Sbiancato

297. Elogiato

298. Ha offerto un eufemismo

299. Valutato

300. Evanesced

301. Evangelized

302. Provato

303. Evocato

304. Evoluto

305. Esacerbato

306. Esaminato

307. Scavato

308. Eccelso

309. Scambiato

310. Detto con enfasi

311. Notato

312. Discolpato

313. Eseguito

314. Esercitato

315. Exhorted

316. Exfoliated

317. Esibito

318. Exonerated

319. Exorcized

320. Espanso

321. Espanso (nel discorso o nella scrittura)

322. Accellerato

323. Con esperienza

324. Spiegato

325. Esplorato

326. Esportato

327. Esposto

328. Espresso

329. Esteso

330. Estrapolato

331. Facilitato

332. Coltivato

333. Faxed

334. Federalized

335. Fertilizzato

336. Archiviato

337. Riempito

338. Filmato

339. Finanziato

340. Infornato

341. Adattare

342. Fisso

343. Oscillato

344. Seguito

345. Previsto

346. Formalizzato

347. Formattato

348. Formato

349. Formulato

350. Fortificato

351. Spedito

352. Trovato

353. Fondato

354. Concessionario

355. Funzionato

356. Ammobiliato

357. Generato

358. Genealogized

359. Geneticized

360. Gesto

361. Firmato dal gesture

362. Girded

363. Gnosticized

364. Governato

365. Classificato

366. Assegnato

367. Rappresentato graficamente

368. Si è sviluppato

369. Garantito

370. Custodito

371. Guidato

372. Hafted

373. Maneggiato

374. Armonizzato

375. Diretto

376. Curativo

377. Aiutato

378. Assunto

379. Umanizzato

380. Humored

381. Hypnotized

382. Identificato

383. Dato fuoco

384. Illustrato

385. Immigrated

386. Impiantato

387. Effettuato

388. Importato

389. Imposto

390. Impressionato

391. Migliorato

392. Incited

393. Incluso

394. Incorporato

395. Aumentato

396. Spostato ad incrementi

397. Indicato

398. Incriminato

399. Industrializzato

400. Influenzato

401. Informed

402. Inizializzato

403. Iniziato

404. Inchiostrato

405. Domandato

406. Controllato

407. Ispirato

408. Installato

409. Istituito

410. Insegnato a

411. Assicurati

412. Integrato

413. Interessato

414. Connesso

415. Interiorizzati

416. Internazionalizzato

417. Interpretato

418. Intervistato

419. Introdotto

420. Intuited

421. Investito

422. Studiato

423. Inventato

424. Inventoried

425. Invertito

426. Investito

427. Corroborato

428. Implicato

429. Pubblicato

430. Unito

431. Registrato

432. Viaggiato

433. Giudicato

434. Juried

435. Giustificato

436. Introdotto

437. Deplorato

438. Laminato

439. Affittato

440. Lanciato

441. Parlato

442. Legalizzato

443. Legitimized

444. Legiferato

445. Diminuito

446. Condotto

447. Di sinistra

448. Illuminato

449. Collegato

450. Contestato

451. Caricato

452. Prestato

453. Localizzato

454. Osservato

455. Lyricized

456. Magnetizzato

457. Spedito

458. Effettuato

459. Controllato

460. Maneggiato

461. Manufactured

462. Di marketing

463. Acquistato padronanza di

464. Misurato

465. Mediato

466. Memorizzato

467. Venduto

468. Fuso

469. Attratto

470. Venuto a contatto di

471. Micrographed

472. Migrato

473. Assistito

474. Moderato

475. Modificato

476. Modellistico

477. Modellato

478. Controllato

479. Variabile

480. Ipotecato

481. Motivato

482. Mosso

483. Trasmesso per radio sul Internet

484. Moltiplicato

485. Mansioni date la priorità a

486. Narrato

487. Traversato

488. Negoziato

489. Trasmesso per radio tramite le reti personali

490. Contatti stabiliti attraverso le reti

491. Neutralizzato

492. Normalizzato

493. Normed

494. Note composte

495. Celebre

496. Informato

497. Notarized

498. Nutrito

499. Verificato

500. Officiated

501. Aperto

502. Comunicato pubblicamente

503. Funzionato

504. Opinioni chieste

505. Disposto

506. Ordinato

507. Organizzato

508. Orientato

509. Iniziato

510. Descritto

511. Oltrepassato

512. Passato

513. Sorpassato

514. Ha funzionato

515. Lucidato

516. Allineato più su

517. Messo in minoranza

518. È diventato più astuto

519. Impressionato

520. Ha sormontato

521. Ha eccessoo

522. Sentito

523. Ha sorvegliato

524. Fatto un passo sopra

525. Allungato

526. Soprafato

527. Sovraccarico

528. Ha scritto sopra

529. Dovuto

530. Posseduto

531. Ossigenato

532. Ossidato

533. Percorso

534. Impaccato

535. Imballato

536. Parented

537. Partecipato

538. Ha unito un'associazione

539. Brevettato

540. Modellato

541. Percepito

542. Effettuato

543. Reso personale

544. Persuaso

545. Fatto una petizione

546. Fotocopiato

547. Fotografato

548. Pilotato

549. Segnato

550. Progettato

551. Piantato

552. Giocato

553. Tracciato

554. Riunito

555. Proposto

556. Inviato

557. Posizionato

558. Esercitato in

559. Pregato

560. Predetto

561. Preempted

562. Introdotto

563. Preferito

564. Preparato

565. Presentato

566. Presieduto

567. Premuto

568. (A) continuati

569. Proceduto

570. Ottenuto

571. Prodotto

572. Professionalized

573. Programmato

574. Proiettato

575. Promosso

576. Proposto

577. Corretto le bozze di

578. Protetto

579. Protestato

580. Prolungato

581. Risultato

582. Fornito

583. Divulg

584. Pubblicato

585. Comprato

586. Qualificato

587. Misurato

588. Accelerato

589. Interrogato

590. Fatto la coda

591. Trapunte progettate

592. Alzato

593. Ha funzionato

594. Rated

595. Realizzato

596. Raccolto

597. Elevato

598. Ragionato

599. Ricordato

600. Ripreso

601. Riconosciuto

602. Suggerito

603. Riconciliato

604. Ricostruito

605. Registrato

606. Recuperato

607. Recuperato

608. Ricreato

609. Reclutato

610. Rettificato

611. Riciclato

612. Riprogettato

613. Redecorated

614. Ridotto

615. Reenacted

616. Rientrato

617. Riferito

618. Rinfrescato

619. Registrato

620. Regolato

621. Rehired

622. Rimborsato

623. Di rinforzo

624. Relativo

625. Liberato

626. Riassegnato

627. Rimediato

628. Ricordato di

629. Ritoccato

630. Rinnovato

631. Affittato

632. Riorientato

633. Riparato

634. Sostituito

635. Riempito

636. Segnalato

637. Rappresentato

638. Richiesto

639. Requisito

640. Ricercato

641. Ridimensionato

642. Rimodellato

643. Risolto

644. Risposto a

645. Ristabilito

646. Resourced

647. Risultato

648. Venduto al dettaglio

649. Mantenuto

650. Riaddestrato

651. Pensionato

652. Lavorato

653. Riaddestrato

654. Richiamato

655. Rinviato

656. Gente portata insieme

657. Migliorato

658. Rivelazioni con esperienza

659. Rivisto

660. Modificato

661. Metallico ancora

662. Aggiornato ai robot

663. Rotolato

664. Ruotato

665. Diretto

666. Scorso veloce

667. Navigato

668. Provato

669. Sterilizzato

670. Risparmiato

671. Esplorato

672. Programmato

673. Notato

674. Selezionato

675. Scrimped

676. Scolpito

677. Ordinato

678. Selezionato

679. Percepito

680. Pubblicato

681. Servito

682. Definisca gli obiettivi

683. Messa a punto

684. Cucito

685. A forma di

686. Compartecipe

687. Tagliuzzato

688. Indicato

689. Semplificato

690. Graduato

691. Venduto

692. Sollecitato

693. Solidificato

694. Risolto

695. Fascicolato

696. Cercato

697. Specificato

698. Spirited

699. Spoke

700. Patrocinato

701. Diffusione

702. Fornito

703. Stabilizzato

704. Standardizzato

705. Starred

706. Dichiato

707. Fatto un passo

708. Sterilizzato

709. Stimolato

710. Raddrizzato

711. Streamlined

712. Rinforzato

713. Allungato

714. Passeggiato

715. Si è sforzato

716. Strutturato

717. Designato

718. Subappaltato

719. Presentati

720. Riuscito

721. Ricapitolato

722. Sorvegliato

723. Fornito

724. Sostenuto

725. Surfed

726. Esaminato

727. Superstite

728. Syndicated

729. Sintetizzato

730. Sistematizzato

731. Tabulato

732. Tamped

733. Insegnato

734. Tassato

735. Funzionato nel paese

736. Telemarketed

737. Telefonato

738. Teletrasmesso

739. Terminato

740. Esaminato

741. Contrastato

742. Detto a

743. Suonato

744. Indurito

745. Fatto un giro di

746. Seguito

747. Rintracciato

748. Commerciato

749. Addestrato

750. Trattato

751. Trascritto

752. Trasferito

753. Tradotto

754. Trasmesso

755. Trasportato

756. Trattato

757. Effettuato un analisi guasti di

758. Carreggiato

759. Troncato

760. Fidato di

761. Scritto

762. Composto

763. Ha intrapreso

764. Unificato

765. Unito

766. Aggiornato

767. Aggiornato

768. Sottolineato

769. Usato

770. Utilizzato

771. Convalidato

772. Vario

773. Venerated

774. Verbalized

775. Verificato

776. Videobiographed

777. Videographed

778. Registrato

779. Osservato

780. Rivendicato

781. Visualizzato

782. Animato

783. Vocalized

784. Espresso

785. Offerto volontariamente

786. Votato

787. Vulcanizzato

788. In attesa

789. Rinunziato a

790. Wassailed

791. Svezzato

792. Pesato

793. Appesantito

794. Saldato

795. Voluto

796. Si è ritirato

797. Comerciato

798. Vinto

799. La parola ha proceduto

800. Funzionato

801. Ha scritto

Action Verbs
German

Action Verbs in German Used
Frequently By Communicators
Tätigkeit Verben: Häufig verwendete Verben für Mitteilende und Karriere-Entwickler

1. Geordnetes____

2. Erklärtes____

3. Festgesetztes____

4. Geplantes____

5. Mitgeteiltes____

6. Konstruiertes____

7. Verursachtes____

8. Entschiedenes____

9. Demonstriertes____

10. Entworfenes____

11. Redigiertes____

12. Angeregtes____

13. Angereichertes____

14. Ausgewertetes____

15. Expatiated____

16. Erfahrenes____

17. Erleichtertes____

18. Eingeführtes____

19. Verbessertes____

20. Erhöhtes____

21. Angezeigtes____

22. Angespornstes____

23. Integriertes____

24. Eingeleitetes____

25. Angewiesenes____

26. Interviewtes____

27. Führendes____

28. Gehörtes____

29. Motiviertes____

30. Verhandeltes____

31. Organisiertes____

32. Geplantes____

33. Vorbereitetes____

34. Produziertes____

35. Gefördertes____

36. Erschienenes____

37. Erforschtes____

38. Repariertes____

39. Korrigiertes___

40. Verkauftes___

41. Überwachtes___

42. Schrieb___

801 Action Verbs in German
Tätigkeit Verben für Mitteilende

1. Herabgesetzt	18. Akklimatisiert
2. Abgekürzt	19. Untergebracht
3. Entzogen	20. Erreicht
4. Geblieben	21. Übereingestimmt
5. Abgeschworen	22. Erklärte
6. Verkürzt	23. Beglaubigt
7. Geabschaffen	24. Angefallen
8. Abseiled	25. Angesammelt
9. Absolviert	26. Gewohnt
10. Enthalten	27. Erzielt
11. Aufgesogen	28. Bestätigt
12. Entzogen	29. Bekannt
13. Angenommen	30. Erworben
14. Beschleunigt	31. Freigesprochen
15. Mit Beifall begrüßt	32. Fungiert
16. Betont	33. Aktiviert
17. Angenommen	34. Verwirklicht

35. Angepaßt

36. Gehaftet

37. Ausgeübt

38. Angenommen

39. Annonciert

40. Geraten

41. Befürwortet

42. Betroffen

43. Bestätigt

44. Geleistet

45. Agented

46. Verbunden

47. Zugestimmt

48. Übereingestimmt

49. Zugeteilt

50. Geändert

51. Analysiert

52. Betäubt

53. Belebt

54. Kommentiert

55. Verkündet

56. Vorweggenommen

57. Gefallene

58. Geerschienene

59. Applaudiert

60. Angewandt

61. Appliquéd

62. Bewertet

63. Anerkannt

64. Vermittelt

65. Archiviert

66. Argumentiert

67. Geordnet

68. Ermittelt

69. Gestrebt

70. Geprüft

71. Zusammengebaut

72. Erklärt

73. Festgesetzt

74. Zugewiesen

75. Angepaßt

76. Unterstützt

77. Verbunden

78. Angenommen

79. Versichert
80. Angebracht
81. Erreicht
82. Beachtet
83. Zugeschrieben
84. Attitudinized
85. Abgestimmt
86. Revidiert
87. Audiodidacted
88. Audiotaped
89. Vergrößert
90. Geschrieben
91. Autorisieren Sie
92. Automatisiert
93. Zugesprochen
94. Wurde
95. Zurückgezogen
96. Bankkonto gehabt
97. Tauschhandel getrieben
98. Wulstig
99. Benchmarked
100. Gefördert

101. Angemeldet
102. Gekauft
103. Umsponnen
104. Brailled
105. Ausgebritten
106. Paniert
107. Übertragen
108. Geholt
109. Geplant
110. Errichtet
111. Errechnet
112. Beruhigt
113. Geworben
114. Kampiert
115. Kardiert
116. Interessiert
117. Getragen
118. Gekarrt
119. Geschnitzt
120. Katalogisiert
121. Katapultiert
122. Zentriert

123. Vorgesessen	145. Gedacht
124. Geändert	146. In den Handel gebracht
125. Gelenkt	147. In Verbindung gestanden
126. Gekennzeichnet	148. Verglichen
127. Aufgeladen	149. Konkurriert
128. Entworfen	150. Kompiliert
129. Gemeißelt	151. Durchgeführt
130. Zitiert	152. Bestanden
131. Zivilisiert	153. Gerechnet
132. Behauptet	154. Automatisiert
133. Erklärt	155. Begriffen
134. Gelöscht	156. Konzentriert
135. Abgestoppt	157. Aufgefaßt
136. Clued	158. Versöhnt
137. Trainiert	159. Geleitet
138. Kodiert	160. Zusammengebaut
139. Kodifiziert	161. Erobert
140. Coifed	162. Konserviert
141. Zusammengearbeitet	163. Betrachtet
142. Gesammelt	164. Konstruiert
143. Gefärbt	165. Analysiert
144. Befohlen	166. Beraten

167. Verbraucht

168. Vertrag abgeschlossen

169. Beigetragen

170. Kontrolliert

171. Zusammengelaufen

172. Unterhalten

173. Zusammengearbeitet

174. Kooptiert

175. Koordinierte

176. Urheberrecht gesichert

177. Geschnürte

178. Behoben

179. Aufeinander bezogen

180. Geraten

181. Gezählt

182. Umworben

183. Verursacht

184. Gutgeschrieben

185. Crewed

186. Critiqued

187. Crusaded

188. Stichwort gegeben

189. Gezüchtet

190. Schnitt

191. Einen Kreislauf durchgemacht

192. Datiert

193. Davened

194. Behandelt

195. Debitiert

196. Debriefed

197. Ausgeprüft

198. Dezentralisiert

199. Entschieden

200. Dechiffroren

201. Deklamiert

202. Erklärt

203. Decodierte

204. Verziert

205. Verringert

206. Engagiert

207. Aufgeschoben

208. Definierte

209. Abgelenkte

210. Beauftragen

211. Gelöscht

212. Abgegrenzt

213. Geliefert

214. Demonstriert

215. Demystified

216. Deprogrammed

217. Gestört

218. Abgeleitet

219. Beschrieben

220. Entworfen

221. Ausführlich

222. Ermittelt

223. Entschlossen

224. Umleitet

225. Sich entwickelt

226. Übergegangen

227. Gespeist

228. Geteilt

229. Erfreut

230. Geplant

231. Gewidmet

232. Bestimmt

233. Dialogiert

234. Gewürfelt

235. Aufgespaltet

236. Vorgeschrieben

237. Unterschieden

238. Verdaut

239. Digitalisiert

240. Verdünnt

241. Verwiesen

242. Digitalisiert

243. Anderer Meinung gewesen

244. Entdeckt

245. Besprochen

246. Zerstreut

247. Angezeigt

248. Aufgelöst

249. Verteilt

250. Geteilt

251. Erahnt

252. Dokumentiert

253. Gespendet

254. Begießst

255. Gezeichnet

256. Fuhr

257. Redigiert

258. Gebildet

259. Bewirkt

260. Effloresced

261. Mühsam erarbeitet aus

262. Ausgearbeitt

263. Elasticized

264. Gestoßen

265. Gewählt

266. Elegized

267. Erhöht

268. Beseitigt

269. Embroided

270. Verbessert

271. Hervorgehoben

272. Beschäftigt

273. Bevollmächtigt

274. Angetroffen

275. Angeregt

276. Angezogen

277. Engagiert

278. Ausgeführt

279. Graviert

280. Erhöht

281. Vergrößert

282. Eingetragen

283. Sichergestellt

284. Hereingekommen

285. Unterhalten

286. Vorgestellt

287. Epigrammatized

288. Abriß gegeben

289. Ausgeglichen

290. Aufgerichtet

291. Eructed

292. Eskortiert

293. Hergestellt

294. Geschätzt

295. Geätzt

296. Etiolated

297. Gepriesen

298. Euphemized

299. Ausgewertet

300. Evanesced

301. Evangelized

302. Bewiesen

303. Erwähnt

304. Entwickelt

305. Verbittert

306. Überprüft

307. Ausgegraben

308. Übertroffen

309. Wert gewesen

310. Ausgerufen

311. Mißbilligt

312. Freigesprochen

313. Durchgeführt

314. Trainiert

315. Exhorted

316. Exfoliated

317. Ausgestellt

318. Entlastet

319. Exorziert

320. Erweitert

321. Expatiated

322. Beschleunigt

323. Erfahren

324. Erklärt

325. Erforscht

326. Exportiert

327. Herausgestellt

328. Ausgedrückt

329. Ausgedehnt

330. Extrapoliert

331. Erleichtert

332. Bewirtschaftet

333. Gefaxt

334. Federalized

335. Befruchtet

336. Eingeordnet

337. Gefüllt

338. Gefilmet

339. Finanziert

340. Abgefeuert

341. Gepaßt

342. Örtlich festgelegt

343. Geschwankt

344. Gefolgt

345. Prognostiziert

346. Formalisiert

347. Formatiert

348. Gebildet

349. Formuliert

350. Verstärkt

351. Nachgeschickt

352. Gefunden

353. Gegründet

354. Franchised

355. Gearbeitet

356. Versorgt

357. Erzeugt

358. Genealogized

359. Geneticized

360. Gestikuliert

361. Gestikuliert

362. Geumgürtet

363. Gnosticized

364. Geregelt

365. Geordnet

366. Bewilligt

367. Graphisch dargestellt

368. Wuchs

369. Garantiert

370. Geschützt

371. Geführt

372. Hafted

373. Angefaßt

374. Harmonisiert

375. Vorangegangen

376. Geheilt

377. Geholfen

378. Angestellt

379. Gevermenschlicht

380. Nachgegeben

381. Hypnotized

382. Gekennzeichnet

383. Angezündet

384. Veranschaulicht

385. Eingewandert

386. Eingepflanzt

387. Eingeführt

388. Importiert

389. Auferlegt

390. Beeindruckt

391. Verbessert

392. Angereizt

393. Enthalten

394. Verbunden

395. Erhöht

396. Registriert

397. Angezeigt

398. Angeklagt

399. Industrialisiert

400. Beeinflußt

401. Informiert

402. Initialisiert

403. Eingeleitet

404. Eingefärbt

405. Erkundigt

406. Kontrolliert

407. Angespornt

408. Angebracht

409. Eingeleitet

410. Angewiesen

411. Versicherte

412. Integriert

413. Interessiert

414. Angeschlossen

415. Internalisierte

416. Internationalisiert

417. Gedeutet

418. Interviewt

419. Eingeführt

420. Intuited

421. Investiert

422. Nachgeforscht

423. Erfunden

424. Inventarisiert

425. Umgekehrt

426. Investiert

427. Belebt

428. Beteiligt

429. Herausgegeben

430. Verbunden

431. Aufgezeichnet

432. Gereist

433. Geurteilt worden

434. Juried

435. Gerechtfertigt

436. Keyboarded

437. Bejammert

438. Lamelliert

439. Gemietet

440. Ausgestoßen

441. Konferiert

442. Legalisiert

443. Legitimiert

444. Gesetze gegeben

445. Vermindert

446. Geführt

447. Link

448. Beleuchtet

449. Verbunden

450. Gestritten

451. Geladen

452. Ausgeliehen

453. Beschränkt

454. Geschauen

455. Lyricized

456. Magnetisiert

457. Verschickt

458. Beibehalten

459. Gehandhabt

460. Manipuliert

461. Hergestellt

462. Vermarktet

463. Erarbeitet

464. Gemessen

465. Vermittelt

466. Gemerkt

467. Verkauft

468. Vermischt

469. Hypnotisiert

470. Getroffen

471. Micrographed

472. Abgewandert

473. Behilflich gewesen

474. Moderiert

475. Geändert

476. Modelliert

477. Geformt

478. Überwacht

479. Verwandelt

480. Hypothekarisch belastet

481. Motiviert

482. Bewogen

483. Multicasted

484. Multipliziert

485. Multitasked

486. Berichtet

487. Gesteuert

488. Vermittelt

489. Netcasted

490. Vernetzt

491. Neutralisiert

492. Normalisiert

493. Normed

494. Notated

495. Gemerkt

496. Mitgeteilt

497. Notariell abgeschlossen

498. Gepflegt

499. Erreicht

500. Amtiert

501. Geöffnet

502. Hat als ein orator gesprochen

503. Funktioniert

504. Gemeint

505. Instrumentiert

506. Bestellt

507. Organisiert

508. Orientiert

509. Entstanden

510. Umrissen

511. Zahlenmäßig überlegen gewesen

512. Outpaced

513. An Leistung geübertroffen

514. Überholt

515. Outshone

516. Outranked

517. Überstimmt

518. Überlistet

519. Overawed

520. Überwand

521. Übertrieb

522. Hörte zufällig

523. Beaufsichtigte

524. Overstepped

525. Overstretched

526. Überwältigt

527. Überarbeitet

528. Überschrieb

529. Schuldig

530. Besessen

531. Oxydiert

532. Oxidiert

533. Geschritten

534. Verpackt

535. Verpackt

536. Parented

537. Teilgenommen

538. Partnered (mit)

539. Patentiert

540. Patterned

541. Wahrgenommen

542. Durchgeführt

543. Personifiziert

544. Überzeugt

545. Ersucht

546. Photokopiert

547. Fotografiert worden

548. Gesteuert

549. Festgelegt

550. Geplant

551. Errichtet

552. Gespielt

553. Geplottet

554. Vereinigt

555. Aufgeworfen

556. Bekanntgegeben

557. In Position gebracht

558. Geübt

559. Gebetet

560. Vorausgesagt

561. Preempted

562. Eingeleitet

563. Bevorzugt

564. Vorbereitet

565. Dargestellt

566. Vorgesessen

567. Betätigt

568. Fortgefahrene (zu)

569. Verarbeitet

570. Verschaffen

571. Produziert

572. Professionalized

573. Programmiert

574. Projiziert

575. Gefördert

576. Vorgeschlagen

577. Korrektur gelesen

578. Geschützt

579. Protestiert

580. Hinausgezogen

581. Geprüft

582. Zur Verfügung gestellt

583. Publiziert

584. Veröffentlicht

585. Gekauft

586. Qualifiziert

587. Quantitativ bestimmt

588. Beschleunigt

589. Gefragt

590. Angestanden

591. Quilted

592. Angehoben

593. Lief

594. Steuerpflichtig

595. Verwirklicht

596. Geerntet

597. Aufgerichtet

598. Gefolgert

599. Zurückgerufen

600. Zurückgefordert

601. Erkannt

602. Empfohlen

603. Versöhnt

604. Wieder aufgebaut

605. Notiert

606. Wieder eingebracht

607. Zurückgewonnen

608. Neu erstellt

609. Eingezogen

610. Korrigiert

611. Aufbereitet

612. Neu entworfen

613. Redecorated

614. Verringert

615. Reenacted

616. Wiederbetreten

617. Bezogen

618. Erneuert

619. Registriert worden

620. Reguliert

621. Rehired

622. Zurückerstattet

623. Verstärkt

624. In Verbindung stehend

625. Freigegeben

626. Verlagert

627. Behoben

628. In Erinnerungen ergangen

629. Umgestaltet

630. Erneuert

631. Gemietet

632. Neuorientiert

633. Repariert

634. Ersetzt

635. Ergänzt

636. Berichtet

637. Dargestellt

638. Erfordert

639. Beansprucht

640. Erforscht

641. Die Größe neu bestimmt

642. Umgestaltet

643. Behoben

644. Reagiert bis

645. Wieder hergestellt

646. Resourced

647. Resultiert

648. Hat im Kleinverkauf gekostet

649. Behalten

650. Retrained

651. Zurückgezogen

652. Retooled

653. Retrained

654. Zurückgeholt

655. Zurückgegangen

656. Gewiedervereinigt

657. Erneuert

658. Hat gefeiert

659. Wiederholt

660. Verbessert

661. Hat verdrahtet

662. Verbessert zu Robotern

663. Gerollt

664. Gedreht

665. Verlegt

666. Gehetzt

667. Gesegelt

668. Probiert

669. Saniert

670. Gespeichert

671. Abgelichtet

672. Festgelegt

673. Gezählt

674. Aussortiert

675. Gespart

676. Gestaltet

677. Der Reihe nach geordnet

678. Vorgewählt

679. Abgefragt

680. Serialized

681. Gedient

682. Stellen Sie Zielsetzungen

683. Ein Stellen Sie

684. Auf Genäht

685. Geformt

686. Geteilt

687. Zerrissen

688. Dargestellt

689. Vereinfacht

690. Sortiert

691. Verkauft

692. Erbeten

693. Verfestigt

694. Gelöst

695. Sortiert

696. Gesucht

697. Spezifiziert

698. Lebhaft

699. Speiche

700. Gefördert

701. Verbreitung

702. Mit Personal versorgt

703. Stabilisiert

704. Standardisiert

705. Hat gehabt die Hauptrolle

706. Angegeben

707. Getreten

708. Entkeimt

709. Angeregt

710. Geradegerichtet

711. Rationalisiert

712. Verstärkt

713. Ausgedehnt

714. Geschlendert

715. Bemühte sich

716. Strukturiert

717. Gestaltet

718. Nebenvertraglich geregelnet

719. Eingereichte

720. Gefolgt

721. Zusammengefaßt

722. Überwacht

723. Geliefert

724. Gestützt

725. Gesurft

726. Überblickt

727. Überlebt

728. Syndicated

729. Synthetisiert

730. Systematisiert

731. Tabelliert

732. Tamped

733. Unterrichtet

734. Besteuert

735. Telecommuted

736. Telemarketed

737. Telephoniert

738. Im Fernsehen übertragen

739. Beendet

740. Geprüft

741. Vereitelt

742. Gesagt

743. Geläutet

744. Abgehärtet

745. Bereist

746. Verfolgt

747. Aufgespürt

748. Gehandelt

749. Ausgebildet

750. Transacted

751. Übertragen

752. Gebracht

753. Übersetzt

754. Übertragen

755. Transportiert

756. Behandelt

757. Überprüft

758. Getauscht

759. Beschnitten

760. Vertraut

761. Geschrieben

762. Gesetzt

763. Nahm sich auf

764. Vereinheitlicht

765. Vereinigt

766. Aktualisiert

767. Verbessert

768. Unterstrichen

769. Verwendet

770. Verwendet

771. Validiert

772. Mannigfaltig

773. Venerated

774. Verbalized

775. Überprüft

776. Videobiographed

777. Videographed

778. Videotaped

779. Angesehen

780. Vindicated

781. Sichtbar gemacht

782. Vitalisiert

783. Vocalized

784. Geäußert

785. Freiwillig erboten

786. Gewählt

787. Vulkanisiert

788. Gewartet

789. Aufgegeben

790. Wassailed

791. Abgesetzt

792. Gewogen

793. Belastet

794. Geschweißt

795. Gewillt

796. Trat zurück

797. Wholesaled

798. Gewonnen

799. Wort verarbeitete

800. Gearbeitet

801. Schrieb

Action Verbs in Portuguese (Brazilian)
Action Verbs Frequently Used by Communicators
Verbos Da Ação: Verbos freqüentemente usados para comunicadores e colaboradores da carreira

1.	___Arranjado	20.	___Aumentado
2.	___Afirmado	21.	___Indicado
3.	___Avaliado	22.	___Inspirado
4.	___Incluído no orçamento	23.	___Integrado
5.	___Comunicado	24.	___Iniciado
6.	___Construído	25.	___Instruído
7.	___Criado	26.	___Entrevistado
8.	___Decidido	27.	___Conduzido
9.	___Demonstrado	28.	___Escutado
10.	___Projetado	29.	___Motivated
11.	___Editado	30.	___Negociado
12.	___Incentivado	31.	___Organizado
13.	___Enriquecido	32.	___De planeamento
14.	___Avaliado	33.	___Preparado
15.	___De Expatiated___	34.	___Produzido
16.	___Experiente	35.	___Promovido
17.	___Facilitado	36.	___Publicado
18.	___Executado	37.	___Pesquisado
19.	___Melhorado	38.	___Reparado

39. ___Revisado

40. ___Vendido

41. ___Supervisionado

42. Escreveu o___

801 Action Verbs in Portuguese (Brazilian)
Verbos da ação para comunicadores

1. Diminuído

2. Abreviado

3. Abstraído

4. Abided

5. Abjurado

6. Abridged

7. Revogado

8. Abseiled

9. Absolved

10. Abstained

11. Absorvido

12. Abstraído

13. Aceitado

14. Acelerado

15. Aclamado

16. Acentuado

17. Aceitado

18. Aclimatado

19. Acomodado

20. Realizado

21. Concordado

22. Explicou

23. Acreditado

24. Resultado

25. Acumulado

26. Accustomed

27. Conseguido

28. Reconhecido

29. Familiar

30. Adquirido

31. Acquitted

32. Agido

33. Ativado

34. Actualized

35.	Adaptado	57.	Aparecidos.
36.	Aderido	58.	Apelados
37.	Administrado	59.	Aplaudido
38.	Adotado	60.	Aplicado
39.	Anunciado	61.	Appliquéd
40.	Recomendado	62.	Appraised
41.	Advogado	63.	Aprovado
42.	Afetado	64.	Arbitrated
43.	Afirmado	65.	Archived
44.	Tido recursos para	66.	Argued
45.	Agented	67.	Arranjado
46.	Agglutinated	68.	Ascertained
47.	Concordado	69.	Aspired
48.	Alinhado	70.	Assayed
49.	Alocado	71.	Montado
50.	Emendado	72.	Afirmado
51.	Analisado	73.	Avaliado
52.	Anesthetized	74.	Atribuído
53.	Animated	75.	Assimilated
54.	Anotado	76.	Ajudado
55.	Anunciado	77.	Associado
56.	Antecipado	78.	Suposto

79. Assegurado
80. Unido
81. Alcançado
82. Atendido
83. Atribuído
84. Attitudinized
85. Attuned
86. Examinado
87. Audiodidacted
88. Audiotaped
89. Aumentado
90. Sido o autor
91. Autorize
92. Automatizado
93. Concedido
94. Tornou-se
95. Suportado
96. Depositado
97. Bartered
98. Frisado
99. Benchmarked
100. Beneficiado

101. Registrado
102. Comprado
103. Trançado
104. Brailled
105. Ramificado
106. Breaded
107. Transmitido
108. Trazido
109. Incluído no orçamento
110. Construído
111. Calculado
112. Acalmado
113. Feito campanha
114. Acampado
115. Carded
116. Importado
117. Carregado
118. Carted
119. Carved
120. Catalogado
121. Catapulted
122. Centrado

123. Chaired

124. Mudado

125. Canalizado

126. Caracterizado

127. Carregado

128. Feito um mapa

129. Cinzelado

130. Cited

131. Civilized

132. Reivindicado

133. Esclarecido

134. Cancelado

135. Cronometrado

136. Clued

137. Treinado

138. Codificado

139. Codified

140. Coifed

141. Collaborated

142. Coletado

143. Colorido

144. Comandado

145. Comemorado

146. Commercialized

147. Comunicado

148. Comparado

149. Competido

150. Compilado

151. Terminado

152. Composto

153. Computado

154. Computarizado

155. Conceived

156. Concentrado

157. Conceptualized

158. Conciliated

159. Conduzido

160. Configurarado

161. Conquistado

162. Conservado

163. Considerado

164. Construído

165. Interpretado

166. Consultado

167. Consumido

168. Contraído

169. Contribuído

170. Controlado

171. Convergido

172. Conversado

173. Cooperado

174. Co-opted

175. Coordenados

176. Copyrighted

177. Corded

178. Corrigido

179. Correlacionado

180. Aconselhado

181. Contado

182. Cortejado

183. Criado

184. Creditado

185. Crewed

186. Critiqued

187. Crusaded

188. Cued

189. Cultivado

190. Corte

191. Dado um ciclo

192. Dated

193. Davened

194. Negociado

195. Debitado

196. Debriefed

197. Eliminado erros

198. Descentralizado

199. Decidido

200. Decifrado

201. Declaimed

202. Declarado

203. Descodificados

204. Decorado

205. Diminuído

206. Dedicado

207. Adiado

208. Delegado

209. Definidos

210. Deflexionados

211. Suprimido

212. Delineado

213. Entregado

214. Demonstrado

215. Demystified

216. Deprogrammed

217. Desregularizado

218. Derivado

219. Descrito

220. Projetado

221. Detalhado

222. Detectado

223. Determinado

224. Detoured

225. Tornado

226. Devolved

227. Jantado

228. Dividido

229. Deleitado

230. Planejado

231. Devotado

232. Diagnosticado

233. Dialogado

234. Cortado

235. Dicotomizado

236. Ditado

237. Diferido

238. Digerido

239. Digitado

240. Diluído

241. Dirigido

242. Digitado

243. Discordado

244. Descoberto

245. Discutido

246. Dispersado

247. Indicado

248. Dissolvido

249. Distribuído

250. Dividido

251. Divined

252. Documentado

253. Doado

254. Doused

255. Esboçado

256. Dirigiu

257. Editado

258. Educado

259. Efetuado

260. Effloresced

261. Eked para fora de

262. Elaborado

263. Elasticized

264. Elbowed

265. Eleito

266. Elegized

267. Elevated

268. Eliminado

269. Embroided

270. Emended

271. Emfatizado

272. Empregado

273. Empowered

274. Encontrado

275. Incentivado

276. Energizado

277. Acoplado

278. Projetado

279. Gravado

280. Realçado

281. Ampliado

282. Alistado

283. Assegurado

284. Entrado

285. Entertained

286. Envisioned

287. Epigrammatized

288. Epitomized

289. Igualado

290. Erigido

291. Eructed

292. Escorted

293. Estabelecido

294. Estimado

295. Gravado

296. Etiolated

297. Eulogized

298. Euphemized

299. Avaliado

300. Evanesced

301. Evangelized

302. Evidenciado

303. Evoked

304. Evoluído

305. Exacerbated

306. Examinado

307. Excavated

308. Excelled

309. Trocado

310. Exclamarado

311. Excoriated

312. Exculpated

313. Executado

314. Exercitado

315. Exhorted

316. Exfoliated

317. Exibido

318. Exonerated

319. Exorcized

320. Expandido

321. Expatiated

322. Expedido

323. Experiente

324. Explicado

325. Explorado

326. Exportado

327. Exposto

328. Expressado

329. Prolongado

330. Extrapolated

331. Facilitado

332. Cultivado

333. Faxed

334. Federalized

335. Fertilized

336. Arquivado

337. Enchido

338. Filmado

339. Financiado

340. Ateado fogo

341. Cabido

342. Fixo

343. Flutuado

344. Seguido

345. Previsto

346. Formalized

347. Formatado

348. Dado forma

349. Formulado

350. Fortified

351. Enviado

352. Encontrado

353. Fundado

354. Franchised

355. Funcionado

356. Fornecido

357. Gerado

358. Genealogized

359. Geneticized

360. Gesticulado

361. Gesticulated

362. Girded

363. Gnosticized

364. Governado

365. Classificado

366. Concedido

367. Representado graficamente

368. Cresceu

369. Garantido

370. Guardado

371. Guiado

372. Hafted

373. Segurado

374. Harmonized

375. Dirigido

376. Healed

377. Ajudado

378. Empregado

379. Humanized

380. Humored

381. Hypnotized

382. Identificado

383. Inflamado

384. Ilustrado

385. Immigrated

386. Implanted

387. Executado

388. Importado

389. Imposto

390. Impresso

391. Melhorado

392. Incited

393. Incluído

394. Incorporado

395. Aumentado

396. Posicionado

397. Indicado

398. Processado

399. Industrialized

400. Influenciado

401. Informed

402. Inicializado

403. Iniciado

404. Coberto

405. Inquirido

406. Inspecionado

407. Inspirado

408. Instalado

409. Instituído

410. Instruído

411. Insured

412. Integrado

413. Interessado

414. Conectarado

415. Internalized

416. Internacionalizado

417. Interpretado

418. Entrevistado

419. Introduzido

420. Intuited

421. Invested

422. Investigado

423. Inventado

424. Inventoried

425. Invertido

426. Invested

427. Avigorado

428. Involvido

429. Emitido

430. Juntado

431. Mantido um diário

432. Viajado

433. Julgado

434. Juried

435. Justificado

436. Keyboarded

437. Lamented

438. Laminado

439. Alugado

440. Lançado

441. Lectured

442. Legalizado

443. Legitimized

444. Legislated

445. Diminuído

446. Conduzido

447. Esquerdo

448. Iluminado

449. Ligado

450. Litigado

451. Carregado

452. Emprestado

453. Localizado

454. Olhado

455. Lyricized

456. Magnetizado

457. Enviado

458. Mantido

459. Controlado

460. Manipulado

461. Manufactured

462. Introduzído no mercado

463. Dominado

464. Medido

465. Mediado

466. Memorizado

467. Merchandised

468. Fundido

469. Mesmerized

470. Encontrado com

471. Micrographed

472. Migrado

473. Ministrado

474. Moderado

475. Modificado

476. Modelado

477. Moldado

478. Monitorado

479. Morphed

480. Mortgaged

481. Motivated

482. Movido

483. Multicasted

484. Multiplicado

485. Multitasked

486. Narrado

487. Navigated

488. Negociado

489. Netcasted

490. Networked

491. Neutralizado

492. Normalizado

493. Normed

494. Notated

495. Notável

496. Notificado

497. Notarized

498. Nutrido

499. Obtido

500. Officiated

501. Aberto

502. Orated

503. Operado

504. Opined

505. Orchestrated

506. Requisitado

507. Organizado

508. Orientado

509. Originado

510. Esboçado

511. Outnumbered

512. Tomado a dianteira

513. Outperformed

514. Outran

515. Outshone

516. Outranked

517. Outvoted

518. Outwitted

519. Overawed

520. Superou

521. Overdid

522. Overheard

523. Oversaw

524. Overstepped

525. Overstretched

526. Oprimido

527. Overworked

528. Overwrote

529. Devido

530. Possuído

531. Oxygenated

532. Oxidado

533. Passeado

534. Empacotado

535. Embalado

536. Parented

537. Participado

538. Partnered (com)

539. Patenteado

540. Modelado

541. Percebido

542. Executado

543. Personalizado

544. Persuadido

545. Peticionado

546. Photocopied

547. Fotografado

548. Pilotado

549. Localizado

550. De planeamento

551. Plantado

552. Jogado

553. Traçado

554. Pooled

555. Posed

556. Afixado

557. Posicionado

558. Praticado

559. Prayed

560. Predito

561. Preempted

562. Prefaciado

563. Preferido

564. Preparado

565. Apresentado

566. Presided

567. Pressionado

568. (A) proseguidos

569. Processado

570. Obtido

571. Produzido

572. Professionalized

573. Programado

574. Projetado

575. Promovido

576. Proposto

577. Corrigido

578. Protegido

579. Protestado

580. Protracted

581. Provado

582. Fornecido

583. Publicized

584. Publicado

585. Comprado

586. Qualificado

587. Quantified

588. Quickened

589. Questionado

590. Enfileirado

591. Quilted

592. Levantado

593. Funcionou

594. Rated

595. Realizado

596. Reaped

597. Elevado

598. Raciocinado

599. Recordado

600. Recuperado

601. Reconhecido

602. Recomendado

603. Reconciled

604. Reconstructed

605. Gravado

606. Recouped

607. Recuperado

608. Recreado

609. Recrutado

610. Retificado

611. Recycled

612. Redesigned

613. Redecorated

614. Reduzido

615. Reenacted

616. Reentered

617. Referenced

618. Refrescado

619. Registado

620. Regulado

621. Rehired

622. Reembolsado

623. Reforçado

624. Relacionado

625. Liberado

626. Relocated

627. Remediado

628. Reminisced

629. Remodelado

630. Renovado

631. Alugado

632. Reoriented

633. Reparado

634. Substituído

635. Reabastecido

636. Relatado

637. Representado

638. Requerido

639. Requisitado

640. Pesquisado

641. Resized

642. Reshaped

643. Resolvido

644. Respondido a

645. Restaurado

646. Resourced

647. Resultado

648. Vendido a varejo

649. Retido

650. Treinado novamente

651. Aposentado

652. Retooled

653. Treinado novamente

654. Recuperado

655. Retornado

656. Reun

657. Revamped

658. Reveled

659. Revisto

660. Revisado

661. Rewired

662. Roboticized

663. Rolado

664. Girado

665. Distribuído

666. Apressado

667. Sailed

668. Provado

669. Sanitized

670. Conservado

671. Feito a varredura

672. Programado

673. Marcado

674. Selecionado

675. Scrimped

676. Sculptured

677. Arranjado em seqüência

678. Selecionado

679. Detetado

680. Colocado em série

681. Servido

682. Ajuste os objetivos

683. Ajuste acima

684. Sewed

685. Dado forma

686. Compartilhado

687. Shredded

688. Mostrado

689. Simplificado

690. Feito sob medida

691. Vendido

692. Solicited

693. Solidified

694. Resolvido

695. Classificado

696. Procurado

697. Especificado

698. Spirited

699. Raio

700. Patrocinado

701. Propagação

702. Staffed

703. Estabilizado

704. Estandardizado

705. Starred

706. Indicado

707. Pisado

708. Sterilized

709. Estimulado

710. Endireitado

711. Aerodinâmico

712. Strengthened

713. Esticado

714. Dado uma volta

715. Strove

716. Estruturado

717. Denominado

718. Subcontracted

719. Submetido

720. Sucedido

721. Sumariado

722. Supervisionado

723. Fornecido

724. Suportado

725. Surfed

726. Examinado

727. Sobrevivido

728. Syndicated

729. Synthesized

730. Systematized

731. Tabulated

732. Tamped

733. Ensinado

734. Taxed

735. Telecommuted

736. Telemarketed

737. Telephoned

738. Televised

739. Terminado

740. Testado

741. Thwarted

742. Dito

743. Anunciado

744. Toughened

745. Excursionado

746. Seguido

747. Seguido

748. Negociado

749. Treinado

750. Transacionado

751. Transcrito

752. Transferido

753. Traduzido

754. Transmitido

755. Transportado

756. Tratado

757. Pesquisado defeitos

758. Transportado

759. Truncado

760. Confiado

761. Datilografado

762. Typeset

763. Empreendeu

764. Unified

765. Unido

766. Updated

767. Promovido

768. Underscored

769. Usado

770. Utilizado

771. Validado

772. Variado

773. Venerated

774. Verbalized

775. Verificado

776. Videobiographed

777. Videographed

778. Gravado

779. Visto

780. Vindicated

781. Visualizado

782. Vitalized

783. Vocalized

784. Expresso

785. Oferecido

786. Votado

787. Vulcanized

788. Esperado

789. Renunciado

790. Wassailed

791. Weaned

792. Pesado

793. Tornado mais pesado

794. Soldado

795. Querido

796. Retirou-se

797. Vendido por atacado

798. Ganhado

799. A palavra processou

800. Trabalhado

801. Escreveu

Action Verbs
Russian

Action Verbs in Russian
Action Verbs Used Frequently by Communicators
Глаголы Действия: Част используемые глаголы для связистов и проявителей карьеры

1. Аранжированное___

2. Утверженное___

3. Определенное___

4. Распланированное___

5. Связываемое___

6. Построенное___

7. Созданное___

8. Решенное___

9. Продемонстрированное___

10. Конструированное___

11. Редактируемое___

12. Ободренное___

13. Обогащенное___

14. Оцененное___

15. ___Expatiated

16. Опытное___

17. Облегченное___

18. Снабженное___

19. Улучшенное___

20. Увеличенное___

21. Показанное___

22. Воодушевлянное___

23. Интегрированное___

24. Начатое___

25. Проинструктированное___

26. Интервьюированное___

27. Водить___

28. Слушаемое___

29. Motivated___

30. Обсуженное___

31. Организованное___

32. Запланированное___

33. Подготовленное___

34. Произведенное___

35. Повышенное___

36. Опубликованное___

37. Исследованное___

38. Отремонтированное___

39. Откорректированное___

40. Проданное___

41. Наблюдали___

42. Написал___

801 Action Verbs in Russian
801 глагол действия на русском языке

1. Притухнуто

2. Сокращено

3. Резюмировано

4. остали

5. Отказанный

6. Сокращенный

7. Аннулированный

8. Спущенный на веревке

9. Освобожденный

10. Воздержано

11. Поглощено

12. Резюмировано

13. Принято

14. Ускорять ход

15. Приветствуемый
(Провозглашенный)

16. Акцентированный

17. Принято

18. Акклиматизировано

19. Приспособлено

20. Accomplished

21. Согласовывано

22. Учл

23. Аккредитировано

24. Увеличивано

25. Аккумулировано

26. Accustomed

27. Достигано

28. Подтвержено

29. Ознакомленный

30. Приобретено

31. Оправданный

32. Подействовано

33. Активировано

34. Актуализировано
35. Приспособлено
36. Придержано
37. Administered
38. Принято
39. Разрекламировано
40. Я советовал
41. Защищено
42. Affected
43. Подтвержено
44. Позволяно
45. Agented
46. Agglutinated
47. Соглашено
48. Выровняно
49. Размещано
50. Откорректировано
51. Проанализировано
52. Анестезировано
53. Одушевляно
54. Аннотировано
55. Объявлено
56. Предвидели
57. Апеллированные
58. Появленные
59. Зааплодировано
60. Прикладной
61. вышитый на шелке
62. Оценено
63. Одобренный
64. Вынесенный решение
65. Архивированный
66. Поспорено
67. Аранжировано
68. Удостоверили в
69. Стремивший
70. измеренный для полезных ископаемых
71. Собрано
72. Утвержено
73. Определено
74. Задано
75. Ассимилировано
76. Помогать

77. Связанный

78. Принято

79. Убежено

80. Прикреплено

81. Достигано

82. Присутствовали на

83. Приписано

84. Позировавший

85. Настроенный

86. Ревизовано

87. самопреподанный

88. Записанный на пленку аудио

89. Увеличено

90. написал как автор

91. Утвердите

92. Автоматизировано

93. Награжено

94. Стал

95. Подперто

96. Накренено

97. Выменяно

98. Украшенный бусами

99. скопированные успешные гиганты

100. Помогано

101. Записано

102. Куплено

103. Braided

104. Brailled

105. Разветвляно

106. Обвалено в сухарях

107. Передано

108. Принесено

109. Распланировано

110. Построено

111. Высчитано

112. Утихомирено

113. Агитировано

114. Расположено лагерем

115. Прочесано

116. Позабочено

117. Снесено

118. Carted

119. Высекано

120. Каталогизировано
121. Катапультировано
122. Центризовано
123. Предводительствовали
124. Изменено
125. Направлено
126. Охарактеризовано
127. Поручено
128. Составлено схему
129. Отделано
130. Процитировано
131. Цивилизовано
132. Востребовано
133. Уточюнено
134. Освобожено
135. Хронометрировали
136. ключ, ход мыслей
137. Я вел
138. Закодировано
139. Составлено кодекс
140. введенные в моду волосы
141. Сотрудничано

142. Собрано
143. Покрашено
144. Управили
145. Commemorated
146. Commercialized
147. Связано
148. Сравнено
149. Состязано
150. Составлено
151. Завершито
152. Составлено
153. Вычислено
154. Компьютеризировано
155. Понято
156. Сконцентрировано
157. Conceptualized
158. Conciliated
159. Дирижировано
160. Установлено
161. Завоевано
162. Сохранено
163. Рассмотрено

164. Построено

165. Construed

166. Посоветовано с

167. Уничтожено

168. Заключено контракт

169. Способствовано

170. Controlled

171. Сойдено

172. Побеседовано

173. Скооперировано

174. Поглощенный

175. Координируемые

176. Авторско прав

177. Связыванные

178. Исправлено

179. Сопоставлено

180. Консультировано

181. Подсчитано

182. Ухаживано

183. Создано

184. Чредитовано

185. Crewed

186. Critiqued

187. Crusaded

188. Намекнуто

189. Выращено в питательноть среде

190. Отрезок

191. Задействовано

192. Dated

193. Davened

194. Общано

195. Оприходовано

196. Обсужено

197. Отлаженный

198. Децентрализовано

199. Решено

200. Расшифровано

201. Протестуемый

202. Объявлено

203. Расшифрованные

204. Украшено

205. Уменьшито

206. Предано

207. Отсрочено

208. Определенные

209. Отклоненные

210. Делегировано

211. Уничтожено

212. Определено

213. Поставлено

214. Продемонстрировано

215. Demystified

216. Deprogrammed

217. Deregulated

218. Выведено

219. Описано

220. Конструировано

221. Детально

222. Обнаружено

223. Определенный

224. измененные(замененные) дороги

225. Превращено

226. переданный

227. Пообедано

228. Разделено

229. Услажено

230. Изобретено

231. Посвященно

232. Диагностировано

233. Dialogued

234. Diced

235. Dichotomized

236. Продиктовано

237. Отличено

238. Усвоино

239. Digitized

240. Разбавлено

241. Сразу

242. Переведенный в цифровую форму

243. не согласил

244. Открыно

245. Обсужено

246. Разметано

247. Показано

248. Растворено

249. Распределено

250. Разделено

251. Предсказывано

252. Документировано

253. Donated

254. Doused

255. Начерчено

256. Управил

257. Отредактировано

258. Educated

259. Произведено эффект

260. Effloresced

261. Eked из

262. Тщательно разработано

263. Elasticized

264. Протолкнуто

265. Избрано

266. Elegized

267. Повышено

268. Исключено

269. Embroided

270. Исправленный

271. Подчеркнуто

272. Использовано

273. Empowered

274. Столкнуто

275. Ободрено

276. Подпитано

277. Включено

278. Проектировано

279. Выгравировано

280. Увеличено

281. Увеличено

282. Завербовано

283. Обеспечено

284. Я вошел

285. Развлечено

286. Envisioned

287. Epigrammatized

288. Epitomized

289. Выравнено

290. Раскрыто

291. изрыгавший

292. Сопровожено

293. Установлено

294. Оценено

295. Вытравлено

296. беливший(побеленный)

297. предлагаемые хвалебные речи

298. Euphemized

299. Оценено

300. Evanesced

301. Evangelized

302. Проявлено

303. Evoked

304. Эволюционировано

305. Exacerbated

306. Рассмотрено

307. Копнуто экскаватором

308. Первенствовано

309. Обменяно

310. Я вскричал

311. жаловавший

312. Оправданный

313. Исполнено

314. Работали

315. Увещано

316. Exfoliated

317. Показанный

318. Реабилитируемый

319. Изгнанный

320. Расширено

321. Разглагольствовавший

322. Ускоряно

323. Опытно

324. Объяснено

325. Исследовано

326. Ехпортировано

327. Подвергли действию

328. Выражено

329. Продленно

330. Экстраполировано

331. Облегчено

332. засеяно

333. Отправлено по факсу

334. Federalized

335. Удобрено

336. Сохранили

337. Заполнено

338. Снято

339. Профинансировано

340. прекращено

341. Приспособлено

342. Фикчировано

343. Изменено

344. Последовано за

345. Прогнозировано

346. Оформлено

347. Форматно

348. Сформировано

349. Сформулировано

350. Укреплено

351. Препровожено

352. Найдено

353. Основано

354. Franchised

355. Задействовано

356. Обеспечено

357. Произведено

358. Genealogized

359. Geneticized

360. жест

361. жестикулировать

362. Опоясано

363. Сделанный гностик

364. Управлено

365. Рассортировано

366. Дарено

367. Изображено

368. Вырос л

369. Гарантировано

370. Защищено

371. Направлено

372. Hafted

373. Отрегулировано

374. Согласовано

375. Возглавлено

376. Излечено

377. Помогли

378. Нанято

379. Гуманизированный

380. веселый

381. Загипнотизировано
382. Определено
383. Воспламенено
384. Проиллюстрировано
385. Immigrated
386. Имплантировано
387. Снабжено
388. Импортировано
389. Наведено
390. Впечатлено
391. Улучшено
392. Подстрекнуто
393. Включенно
394. Включено
395. Увеличено
396. Индексировано
397. Показано
398. Предъявлено обвинение
399. Индустриализировано
400. Повлияно на
401. информированный
402. Выступлено с иничиативой

403. Начато
404. Покрыно краской
405. Запрошено
406. Проверено
407. Воодушевляно
408. Установлено
409. Учрежено
410. Проинструктировано
411. Insured
412. Интегрировано
413. Заинтересовано
414. Взаимодействовали
415. Внедренные
416. Интернационализировано
417. Интерпретировано
418. Интервьюировано
419. Введено
420. Intuited
421. Проинвестировано
422. Расследовано
423. Изобретено
424. Inventoried

425. Перевернуто

426. Проинвестировано

427. подбодренный

428. вовлеченный

429. Выдано

430. Соединено

431. записанный в журнал

432. Путешествовано

433. Рассужено

434. судивший

435. Оправдано

436. Keyboarded

437. Посетовано

438. Прокатано

439. Арендовано

440. Запущено

441. Прочитано лекцию

442. Узаконено

443. Legitimized

444. Законодательствовано

445. Lessened

446. Водить

447. Лево

448. Освещено

449. Соединено

450. Litigated

451. Нагружено

452. Одолжено

453. Локализовано

454. Посмотрено

455. написал песни

456. Намагничено

457. Переслано

458. Поддержано

459. Управили

460. Манипулировано

461. Изготовлено

462. О на рынок

463. Управили

464. Измерено

465. Посредничано

466. Запомнено

467. Торговано

468. Слито

469. Загипнотизированный

470. Встрещено

471. Micrographed

472. Проникли

473. Послужено

474. Умерено

475. Доработано

476. Моделировано

477. Отлито в форму

478. Проконтролировано

479. измененный(замененный)

480. Заложено

481. мотивируемый

482. Двинуто

483. Радиопередача на Интернете

484. Умножено

485. расположенные по
     приоритетам задачи

486. Повествовано

487. Проведенный

488. Обсужено

489. Интернет передал по радио

490. Networked

491. Нейтрализовано

492. Нормализованный

493. Normed

494. написал примечания

495. Замечено

496. Сообщено

497. Notarized

498. Вынянчено

499. Получено

500. Исполненный обязанности

501. Раскрыно

502. Разглагольствовавший

503. Работали

504. Полагавший

505. Оркестровано

506. Приказано

507. Организовано

508. Ориентировано

509. Возникли

510. Конспектировано

511. Превзойденный численностью

512. Опережаемый

513. Побежденный

514. Опережал

515. Затменный

516. оцениваемый выше

517. забаллотированный

518. перехитривший

519. Вызванный благоговение

520. Отжал

521. Переусердствовал

522. Подслушал

523. Надзирал

524. Переступленный

525. Сверхпротянутый

526. Разбитый

527. Переутомленный

528. Переписывал

529. Одолженно

530. Имели

531. Оксигенировано

532. Окислено

533. Шагнуто

534. Упаковано

535. Упаковано

536. Parented

537. Участвовали

538. полученный партнер

539. Запатентовано

540. Сделано по образцу

541. Воспринимано

542. Выполнено

543. Персонализировано

544. Уговорено

545. Урезонено

546. Photocopied

547. Сфотографировано

548. Пилотировали

549. Pinpointed

550. Запланировано

551. Засажено

552. Сыграно

553. Прокладывать курс

554. Сложено вместе

555. Представлено

556. Вывешено

557. Расположено

558. Напрактиковано

559. Помолено

560. Предсказано

561. Выгружаемый
(Резервируемый)

562. Предпослано

563. Предпочесно

564. Подготовлено

565. Представлено

566. Председательствовано

567. Отжато

568. Продолжаемые (к)

569. Обработано

570. Выхлопотано

571. Произведено

572. Профессионал

573. Запрограммировано

574. Запроектировано

575. Повышено

576. Предложено

577. Доказательство читает

578. Защищено

579. Опротестовано

580. Длительный

581. Доказано

582. Обеспечено

583. Разглашенный

584. Опубликовано

585. Закуплено

586. Квалифицировано

587. Квантифицировано

588. Ускоренный

589. Спрошено

590. С очередями

591. Выстегано

592. Поднято

593. Побежал

594. Номинальный

595. Осуществляно

596. Поужинано

597. Поднято

598. Размышляли

599. Вспомнено

600. Исправленный

601. Узнано

602. Порекомендовано

603. Примирено

604. Реконструировано

605. Записано

606. Возмещаемый

607. Взято

608. Воссоздано

609. Завербовано

610. Выпрямлено

611. Рециркулировано

612. Переконструировано

613. Ремонтировавший

614. Уменьшено

615. Повторно предписанный

616. Перевведенный

617. Снабжено ссылками

618. Освежено

619. Зарегистрировано

620. Отрегулировано

621. Повторно нанятый

622. Возмещено

623. Усилено

624. Родствено

625. Выпущено

626. Передислоцировано

627. Исправлено

628. Reminisced

629. Remodeled

630. Возобновлено

631. Арендовано

632. Переориентировано

633. Отремонтировано

634. Заменено

635. Пополнено

636. Сообщено

637. Представлено

638. Потребовано

639. Реквизировано

640. Исследовано

641. Измененный размеры

642. Переформовано

643. Разрешено

644. Отвечено до

645. Восстановлено

646. Resourced

647. Приведено к

648. О в розницу

649. Сохранено

650. Переучено

651. Выбыто

652. Переоборудованный

653. Переучено

654. Восстановленный

655. Возвращено

656. Воссоединено

657. Обновляемый

658. знаменитый

659. Рассмотрено

660. Откорректировано

661. Перезашитый

662. Модернизированный на роботы

663. Свернуто

664. Вращано

665. Направлено

666. Поспешено

667. Sailed

668. Попробовано

669. Санировано

670. Сохранено

671. Просмотрено

672. Запланировано

673. улучшил мой счет

674. Экранировано

675. урезанный

676. Изваяно

677. вставьте последовательность

678. Выбрано

679. Воспринято

680. Издано сериями

681. Послужено

682. Установите задачи

683. Установите вверх

684. Зашито

685. Сформировано

686. Поделено

687. разорвал

688. Показано

689. Упрощано

690. Определено размер

691. Продано

692. Ходатайствовано

693. Затвердето

694. Разрешено

695. Сортировано

696. Изыскано

697. Определено

698. энергичный

699. Спица

700. Спонсировано

701. Распространение

702. Укомплектовано штаты

703. Стабилизировано

704. Унифицировано

705. усеянный звездами

706. Заявлено

707. Шагнуто

708. Простерилизовано

709. Простимулировано

710. Выправлено

711. Упрощенный

712. Усилено

713. Протягивано

714. Погуляно

715. Устремил

716. Составлено

717. Введено в моду

718. Подзаконтрактованный

719. Представленные

720. Преуспето

721. Суммировано

722. Наблюдали

723. Поставлено

724. Поддержано

725. Прибо

726. Произведено съемку

727. Выдержано

728. посланный синдикату

729. Синтезировано

730. Систематизировано

731. Приведено

732. Утрамбовано

733. Научено

734. Таксировано

735. работавший дома

736. Telemarketed

737. Телефонировано

738. Передано телепрограмму

739. Прекращено

740. Испытано

741. Мешавший

742. Сказано

743. Позвонено

744. Ужесточенный

745. Путешествовано

746. Трассировано

747. Отслежено

748. Торговано

749. Натренировано

750. проведенный

751. Транскрибировано

752. Перенесено

753. Переведено

754. Передано

755. Транспортировано

756. Обработано

757. Устранено неисправность:

758. Перевезли на грузовиках

759. Усечено

760. Доверено

761. Напечатано на машинке

762. Набранный

763. Предпринял

764. Унифицировано

765. Соединено

766. Обновленный

767. Модернизировано

768. Подчеркнутый

769. Использовано

770. Использовано

771. Утвержено

772. Varied

773. уважавший

774. Разглагольствовавший

775. Подтвержено

776. Видео записало на пленку биографии

777. записанный на пленку видео биография

778. Снятый

779. Осмотрено

780. Доказанный

781. Визуализировано

782. Оживляемый

783. Напевавший

784. Выражено

785. работать для свободно

786. Проголосовано

787. Вулканизировано

788. остали

789. Отклоненный

790. облюдаемый(оплаченный, чтимый,удостоенный)

791. Отнятый от груди

792. Весили

793. Утяжелено

794. Сварено

795. Завещано

796. Разделил

797. Продано оптом

798. Выиграно

799. Слово обрабатывало

800. Работать

801. Написал

Index

Frequently Used Action Verbs

Communicators' Action Verbs

Franchised, 11, 33, 55, 77, 99, 121, 143

Functioned, 11, 33, 55, 77, 99, 121, 143

Furnished, 11, 33, 55, 77, 99, 121, 143

Generated, 11, 33, 55, 77, 99, 121, 143

Genealogized, 11, 33, 55, 77, 99, 121, 143

Geneticized, 11, 33, 55, 77, 99, 121, 143

Gestured, 11, 33, 55, 77, 99, 121, 143

Gesticulated, 11, 33, 55, 77, 99, 121, 143

Girded, 11, 33, 55, 77, 99, 121, 143

Gnosticized, 11, 33, 55, 77, 99, 121, 143

Governed, 11, 33, 55, 77, 99, 121, 143

Graded, 11, 33, 55, 77, 99, 121, 143

Granted, 11, 33, 55, 77, 99, 121, 143

Graphed, 11, 33, 55, 77, 99, 121, 143

Grew, 11, 33, 55, 77, 99, 121, 143

Guaranteed, 11, 33, 55, 77, 99, 121, 143

Guarded, 11, 33, 55, 77, 99, 121, 143

Guided, 11, 33, 55, 77, 99, 121, 143

Hafted, 11, 33, 55, 77, 99, 121, 143

Handled, 11, 33, 55, 77, 99, 121, 143

Harmonized, 11, 33, 55, 77, 99, 121, 143

Headed, 11, 33, 55, 77, 99, 121, 143

Healed, 11, 33, 55, 77, 99, 121, 143

Helped, 11, 33, 55, 77, 99, 121, 143

Hired, 11, 33, 55, 77, 99, 121, 143

Humanized, 11, 33, 55, 77, 99, 121, 143

Humored, 11, 33, 55, 77, 99, 121, 143

Hypnotized, 11, 33, 55, 77, 99, 121, 144

Identified, 11, 33, 55, 77, 99, 121, 144

Ignited, 11, 33, 55, 77, 99, 121, 144

Illustrated, 11, 33, 55, 77, 99, 121, 144

Immigrated, 11, 33, 56, 77, 99, 121, 144

Implanted, 11, 33, 56, 77, 99, 121, 144

Implemented, 11, 34, 56, 78, 100, 122, 144

Imported, 11, 34, 56, 78, 100, 122, 144

Imposed, 11, 34, 56, 78, 100, 122, 144

Impressed, 11, 34, 56, 78, 100, 122, 144

Improved, 11, 34, 56, 78, 100, 122, 144

Incited, 11, 34, 56, 78, 100, 122, 144

Included, 11, 34, 56, 78, 100, 122, 144

Incorporated, 11, 34, 56, 78, 100, 122, 144

Increased, 12, 34, 56, 78, 100, 122, 144

Indexed, 12, 34, 56, 78, 100, 122, 144

Indicated, 12, 34, 56, 78, 100, 122, 144

Indicted, 12, 34, 56, 78, 100, 122, 144

Industrialized, 12, 34, 56, 78, 100, 122, 144

0-595-31911-4